New Leadership Imperatives

Inspiring the Next Game: Strategy Ideas for Forward Looking Leaders

BCG Henderson Institute

New Leadership Imperatives

Edited by
Martin Reeves

DE GRUYTER

ISBN 978-3-11-077508-2
e-ISBN (PDF) 978-3-11-077517-4
e-ISBN (EPUB) 978-3-11-077520-4
ISSN 2701-8857

Library of Congress Control Number: 2022938191

Bibliographic information published by the Deutsche Nationalbibliothek
The Deutsche Nationalbibliothek lists this publication in the Deutsche Nationalbibliografie;
detailed bibliographic data are available on the internet at http://dnb.dnb.de.

© 2022 The BCG Henderson Institute
Cover image: sesame/DigitalVision Vectors/Getty Images
Typesetting: Integra Software Services Pvt. Ltd.
Printing and binding: CPI books GmbH, Leck

www.degruyter.com

Acknowledgments

We would like to acknowledge all of the authors whose work appears on the following pages: Michelle Akers, Allison Bailey, Elena Barybkina, Vikram Bhalla, Stephen Bungay, Andrew Cainey, François Candelon, Tom Deegan, Anson Dorrance, Diana Dosik, Andrew Dyer, C. Patrick Erker, Gerry Hansell, Johann D. Harnoss, Fabien Hassan, Georg Kell, Mathieu Lefèvre, Sandy Moose, Martin Reeves, Joshua Serlin, Jeff Sullivan, Peter Tollman, Roselinde Torres, Christian Veith and Kevin Whitaker.

We would also like to acknowledge the broader BCG Henderson Institute community: our Fellows, Ambassadors, and operations teams over the years, who have all made invaluable contributions to our research; our academic collaborators, who have expanded our horizons of new ideas; and our BCG practice area partners, who have collaborated with us on several of these articles.

https://doi.org/10.1515/9783110775174-202

About the BCG Henderson Institute

The BCG Henderson Institute is the Boston Consulting Group's think tank, dedicated to exploring and developing valuable new insights from business, technology, economics, and science by embracing the powerful technology of ideas. The Institute engages leaders in provocative discussion and experimentation to expand the boundaries of business theory and practice and to translate innovative ideas from within and beyond business.

https://doi.org/10.1515/9783110775174-203

Contents

Part I: The Modern Role of Leadership

Part II: Leadership Lessons

Introduction

Leaders face a broad variety of challenges in an organization at any given time. These challenges range from establishing strategic goals to ensuring businesses reach their full potential to engaging customers and other stakeholders. As we have seen with the COVID-19 crisis, these responsibilities become even more complex in a crisis – when employees and stakeholders turn to business leaders for direction. Moreover, amid social and geopolitical uncertainty, business leaders are increasingly being pressured to weigh in on a growing number of social and political issues.

Today's business climate creates new challenges and requires new approaches to leadership. Some existing leaders will rise to the occasion, while others will struggle to adapt. What will successful leadership require in the coming decade?

Leadership roles change based on the situation of the organization – through digital transformations, crises, renewals, and other challenges. In Part I of this book, we discuss the modern role of leadership.

Chapter 1, "Leadership Matters: When, How Much, and How?" dives into just how much impact CEOs have on company performance and what separates top-performing CEOs from the rest.

Chapter 2, "The Board's Role in Strategy in a Changing Environment," details the challenges that directors face, the capabilities they can bring to the table, and the best practices of forward-looking companies when it comes to the board's role in strategy.

Chapter 3, "A Lot Will Change – So Must Leadership," discusses four imperatives for leaders as they transform their companies to become "bionic," as technology reshapes organizations.

Chapter 4, "When Leadership Matters Most," outlines several common leadership traps across organizations, as well as guiding principles that leaders need to heed during a crisis.

Chapter 5, "Fostering Organizational Stamina," covers how leaders can address a rising sentiment of impatience and foster the stamina required for organizations to successfully adapt to new conditions.

To succeed over the long run, business leaders can no longer rely exclusively on traditional approaches to business management; they must learn from other fields as well. Part II of this book discusses leadership lessons drawn from different individuals and areas of expertise – from the military to sports to psychology to neuroscience.

https://doi.org/10.1515/9783110775174-205

Chapter 6, "Lessons in Leadership from the Great Commanders," explores how leaders can learn a great deal from the great military commanders of history.

Chapter 7, "The Rewards of CEO Reflection," shows how by routinely setting aside time in their calendars, CEOs can reap the rewards of reflection.

Chapter 8, "A CEO's Guide to Leading and Learning in the Digital Age," explores building a learning ecosystem that elevates learning strategy to the CEO level and embraces new digital possibilities.

Chapter 9, "The Power of Inspiration, Perspiration, and Cooperation – In Sports and in Business," looks at the performance of sports teams to show how other organizations can promote cooperation and improve performance.

Organizations do not operate in a vacuum but rather in a dynamic environment that they both influence and are influenced by. Part III concludes by discussing the evolving challenges leaders will face as they lead in this new environment with issues ranging from social polarization to geopolitical instability.

Chapter 10, "The Business of Business Is No Longer Just Business," discusses the relationship between business and other parts of society, and the profound implications for strategy and competitive advantage.

Chapter 11, "The Case for Corporate Statesmanship," makes the case for CEOs to take a bolder role in addressing some of society's major issues.

Chapter 12, "Mind the Gap: Navigating the New Fault Lines of Global Business," covers how multinationals, with business models built on operating across borders, can navigate the shifting geopolitical environment.

Chapter 13, "In Sync: Unlocking Collective Action in a Connected World," looks at how to leverage digital technologies to increase reach, speed, and ease of collective action.

Chapter 14, "How Business Leaders Can Reduce Polarization," offers 12 actions that CEOs can take to effectively reduce division and protect their businesses in increasingly polarized times.

In a world in which the role of a leader and the business environment are always changing, we hope this book will guide leaders in making the right choices for their organizations, their stakeholders, and society as a whole.

Part I: **The Modern Role of Leadership**

Martin Reeves, Peter Tollman, Gerry Hansell, Kevin Whitaker,
Tom Deegan

Chapter 1
Leadership Matters: When, How Much, and How?

CEOs face a host of challenges in even the best of times, from setting strategic direction, to ensuring the organization is reaching its full potential, and engaging internal and external stakeholders effectively – all while assuming accountability for performance and serving as the company's main spokesperson. These responsibilities become even more complex in times of crisis like the COVID-19 pandemic, as employees and stakeholders turn to CEOs for direction, information, and motivation.

With such a spotlight on leadership, it's worth stepping back and understanding the role that CEOs play in driving company performance. Just how much impact do CEOs have on their firms? How is this shaped by the context? And what separates top-performing CEOs from the rest?

To answer these questions, we have studied the tenures of 7,000 CEOs worldwide to identify how much and how they affected their companies' performance trajectories. We looked at the sustained effect of each CEO on their firm's Total Shareholder Return (TSR) relative to peers, controlling for the year, industry, and prior firm performance (see Box 1.1 for detailed methodology).

In summary, our research shows:

1. New CEOs often cause a significant, sustained change in their company's outperformance. The top 20% of CEOs outperformed their sector by +9 percentage points per year over the course of their tenure, controlling for other factors; whereas the bottom 20% underperformed by –11 percentage points.

2. The spread of CEO impact varies by strategic context. The gap between the most successful and unsuccessful CEOs is up to 9 percentage points wider in fast-growing, technology driven businesses compared to slower-growing, more regulated contexts.

3. The CEO effect tends to decline with scale. The spread caused by the CEO effect is greater among smaller firms (driven largely by higher potential upside), but a significant performance spread exists in companies of all sizes.

https://doi.org/10.1515/9783110775174-001

4. Some actions are associated with CEO success across nearly all contexts. Top-performing CEOs are more likely to take a long-term approach to strategy, accelerate M&A (mergers and acquisitions) activity, increase their company's ESG (environmental, social, and governance) scores, and pay more attention to diversity.

5. Others are associated with success only in specific contexts. For example, when taking on a severely underperforming company, CEOs are more likely to be successful if they change out more of their reports. Additionally, among leaders who launched corporate transformations during their tenure, those that did so in the first or second year outperformed those who waited longer.

6. Most personal CEO traits (including hire type, prior CEO experience, gender, age, and education) have no impact on *average* performance. However, they can affect the risk profile – for example, external hires have a greater spread of outcomes.

7. Personality has a limited impact on success. Based on an outside-in assessment of CEOs' personality traits made using natural language processing techniques, we observe that no profile guarantees or precludes success.

Box 1.1: Details on Methodology

We analyzed CEOs listed in BoardEx's database that led companies with at least $50 million in inflation-adjusted sales between 1985 and 2018. CEOs were excluded if they did not stay at the company for at least three years.

To estimate the CEO effect, we built a model regressing annual TSR outperformance on control variables for year, industry, and starting position, as well as an indicator variable for each CEO. We control for year and industry using indicator variables for each year and industry average outperformance for each year-industry pair. To control for prior firm performance, we use two-year trailing average TSR outperformance prior to the start of the CEO's tenure. To remove the impact of extreme outliers, the top and bottom 5% of TSR outperformance are winsorized.

The value of the coefficients for each CEO indicator variable then represent the "CEO effect" or the sustained, annual impact on TSR outperformance throughout a CEO's tenure.

Analyzing the CEO Effect

New CEO tenures often mark a sustained change in firm performance. The best among them, defined as those with a top-quintile CEO effect, positively impact

TSR outperformance by at least +9 percentage points annually throughout their tenure. Consider Satya Nadella, Microsoft's CEO since 2014. Faced with Windows' declining market share, Nadella accelerated Microsoft's shift to a cloud-based business model and completed several major acquisitions. Controlling for the company's sector and starting position, Nadella has had a positive impact of +16 percentage points annually throughout his tenure (see Figure 1.1).

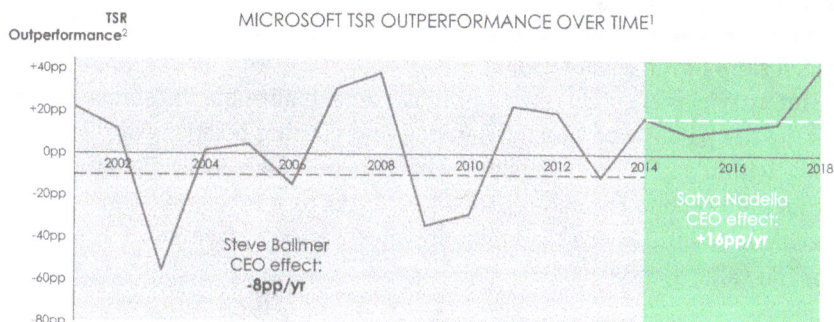

MICROSOFT TSR OUTPERFORMANCE OVER TIME[1]

TSR Outperformance[2]

Steve Ballmer CEO effect: -8pp/yr

Satya Nadella CEO effect: +16pp/yr

1. CEO effect also controls for year, sector, and prior trajectory, so CEO effect will not exactly match average TSR outperformance
2. Annual TSR outperformance compared to sector median
Source: S&P Global, BCG Henderson Institute analysis

Figure 1.1: A high CEO effect demonstrates consistent outperformance.

Haishan Liang of Haier Smart Home is another example. As CEO of the smart home products manufacturer, Liang grew the firm's IoT (Internet of Things) data ecosystem by entering a strategic partnership with Baidu, acquired GE Appliances in 2016, and renamed and repositioned the firm as the orchestrator of a home device ecosystem. Since the start of Liang's tenure in 2013, the firm's market capitalization has more than doubled.

Some CEO tenures, however, are marked by a similarly strong negative impact on firm performance. CEOs in the bottom quintile have a –11 percentage point impact annually, after adjusting for other factors.

We can express the overall impact of CEO leadership as *the spread between the effects of the best and worst-performing CEOs* – in other words, the sustained change in firm outperformance over the course of their tenure, controlling for starting position and other factors. Overall, the spread between top- and bottom-quintile CEOs is 20 percentage points per year – which, over the median CEO tenure of six years, accumulates to a gap larger than the starting enterprise value of the company.

However, the impact that a CEO tenure has on firm performance varies by context. As an example, the CEO impact is generally larger in dynamic, fast-growing sectors. CEOs in IT, communications services (including internet services), and consumer discretionary (including digital entertainment and internet retail) have the widest spread in CEO impact (23 points). In contrast, in more regulated and slower growing industries (real estate, utilities, and financials), CEOs have a narrower spread of impact (14–17 points). This may reflect the fact that faster-growing environments are more malleable[1] – leaders can more easily shape the future direction of the market – whereas CEOs' actions are more constrained in highly regulated or slow growth environments.

Industry classifications may not fully contextualize the CEO impact, however, as the patterns of value generation and starting positions of firms vary widely within and across industries. This is increasingly so as digital technology facilitates competition and collaboration across industries. Our prior research has identified the ten common value patterns[2] (see Box 1.2 for more detail on value patterns).

Box 1.2: Details on Value Patterns

While each company's starting context is unique, past empirical research of recurring common patterns points to ten distinct archetypes, or value patterns, that describe the set of performance priorities most aligned with value creation[3] (see Figure 1.2).

When analyzing by these distinct value patterns, a similar paradigm emerges. CEOs have the largest impact when they take on the leadership of companies in high-growth, technologically intensive contexts. CEOs inheriting firms with *Healthy High Growth* and *Asset-Light Services* value patterns have the largest spread in CEO impact (23–25 percentage points). In contrast, CEOs tend to have less impact when inheriting *High Value Brands*, which are characterized by generating stable returns from established brand assets, and *Discovery* firms, which are characterized by long cycle, bottom-up innovation.

Another factor that affects the CEO impact is the size of an organization. Among the largest companies in our sample, those with $50 billion+ in annual inflation-adjusted revenue, the spread between top- and bottom-quintile CEO

---

1 https://www.bcg.com/publications/collections/your-strategy-needs-strategy/intro.

2 https://www.bcg.com/publications/2012/value-creation-strategy-corporate-strategy-portfolio-management-value-patterns.

3 For more information, see BCG'S article on "Value Patterns: The Concept." https://www.bcg.com/publications/2012/value-creation-strategy-corporate-strategy-portfolio-management-value-patterns.

Value Pattern	Overview	Example
Healthy High Growth	Category innovators, high growth and valuation, low debt	Amazon.com, Inc.
Discovery	R&D intensive, medium growth, very high valuation	Microsoft Corp.
High Value Brands	Advantaged offering in mature categories, stable margins	The Walt Disney Company
Asset-Light Services	Service/ product aggregators, asset light, high valuations	Costco Wholesale Corp.
Asset-Heavy Discovery	Capital-intensive innovators, high margins and volatility	Intel Corporation
Average (Diversified)	Heterogeneous, average volatility and valuation	Walmart, Inc.
Hard Assets	Capacity operators in cyclical industries, some debt leverage	AT&T Inc.
Utility-like	Capacity operators in stable industries, high debt leverage	Toyota Motor Corporation
Deep Value	Undifferentiated competitors, some debt leverage (~15%)	Kia Motors Corp.
Distressed	Very capital intensive, high debt leverage (~50%)	J.C. Penney Company, Inc.

Figure 1.2: Details on value pattern.

effects is 15 percentage points, whereas companies with \$5–50 billion in revenue have a spread of 17 points, and the smallest companies have an even greater spread. This is driven by higher upside for top-quintile CEOs in smaller companies; the downside of underperforming CEOs is similar across size groups. This reflects the fact that extraordinary returns are more likely to be generated from a smaller base, as well as the fact that sustainable reinvention becomes harder as companies age and grow.[4]

Finally, if history is any guide, the current crisis period may be accompanied by a wave of new CEOs – it is perhaps no surprise that the financial crisis of 2008 also saw a peak in CEO turnover, with nearly 20% of leaders departing that year. Evidence shows that the impact of CEOs' performance rose slightly in the last two downturns, driven more by a greater downside for underperforming leaders. However, the upside for top CEOs remained just as high as in other circumstances, in terms of their impact on relative outperformance, reminding us that advantage can be found in adversity.[5]

For example, Jim Whitehurst took over RedHat at the start of the last recession. With IT budgets slashed, corporate customers, initially wary of the shift away from familiar enterprise solutions, gave RedHat's less expensive open-source solutions a second look. Under Whitehurst, RedHat capitalized on this opportunity – signing up customers for longer-term deals and investing in emerging technologies such as cloud computing and virtualization. As a result, RedHat emerged from the global financial crisis with double-digit revenue growth, a trend it continued until its acquisition in 2019 by IBM.

Identifying Success Factors for CEO Leadership

Given the sustained impact that CEOs can have on their companies' trajectories (for better or for worse), it is important to know how they can tilt the odds in their favor. By using financial and non-financial signals to identify the different moves that CEOs have made, we can identify which factors set successful leaders apart from unsuccessful ones.

A few success factors are associated with high CEO performance across all contexts:

---

4 https://www.bcg.com/publications/2019/achieving-vitality-in-turbulent-times.
5 https://www.bcg.com/publications/2019/advantage-in-adversity-winning-next-downturn.

1. They take a long-term, externally oriented approach to strategy. The top performing CEOs drive excellence in strategic thinking. Based on a proprietary natural language processing analysis of SEC filings and annual reports, our research indicates that top CEOs preside over organizations which stand apart from peers on several dimensions: long-term orientation, which indicates a strategic focus on the firm's future as well as the present; "biological thinking,"[6] a measure of the adaptiveness, flexibility, and mutualism best-suited for a complex and dynamic business environment; and a focus on purpose, an approach to strategy that extends beyond financial performance and matches a firm's capabilities and aspirations with societal needs (see Figure 1.3).

Median strategy score during CEOs' tenure[1]

Long-term orientation	'Biological' orientation	Purpose focus

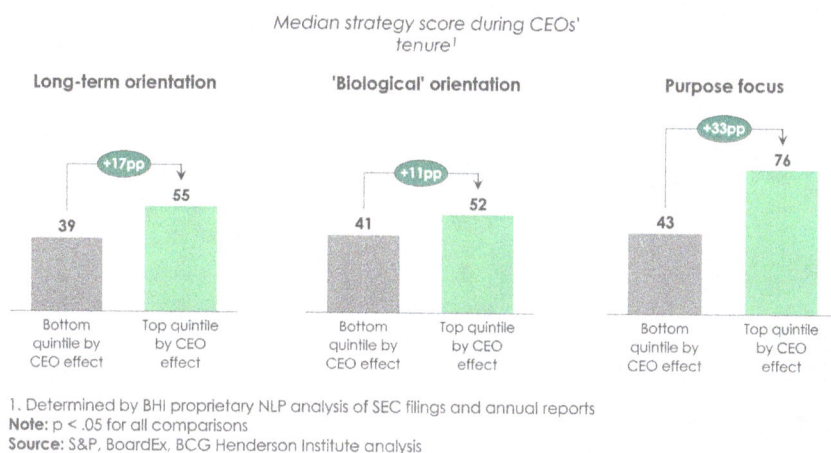

1. Determined by BHI proprietary NLP analysis of SEC filings and annual reports
Note: p < .05 for all comparisons
Source: S&P, BoardEx, BCG Henderson Institute analysis

Figure 1.3: Strategic orientation of best- and worst-performing CEOs.

One such CEO is Kasper Rorsted of Adidas AG. As CEO, Rorsted has embraced a long-term strategic orientation, emphasizing that the key to Adidas' global sourcing model is its long-term relationships with suppliers.[7] At the end of 2018, 84% of their strategic suppliers had worked with Adidas for more than 10 years and 42% for over 20 years. Since the start of 2016, Rorsted has had a positive annual impact of +25 percentage points on outperformance.

---

6 https://www.bcg.com/publications/2017/think-biologically-messy-management-for-complexworld.

7 https://www.adidas-group.com/en/sustainability/managing-sustainability/human-rights/supply-chain-approach/.

2. They accelerate M&A activity. Relative to their predecessors, top-quintile CEOs accelerated acquisition activity by an average of 15% throughout their tenure. Bottom-quintile CEOs, in contrast, decelerated acquisition activity by an average of 7%. While poor-performing CEOs tend to immediately decelerate M&A, successful CEOs, in contrast, tend to initially maintain a similar level of deal activity as that of their predecessor. Then, having gained license to do more, they accelerate and sustain elevated levels of deal activity. This suggests successful CEOs take a more activist approach to capital allocation (see Figure 1.4).

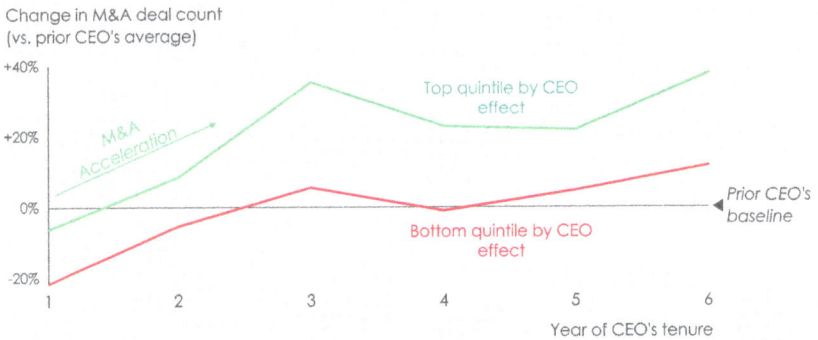

Change in M&A deal count
(vs. prior CEO's average)

+40%

Top quintile by CEO effect

+20%

M&A Acceleration

0%

Prior CEO's baseline

Bottom quintile by CEO effect

-20%

1   2   3   4   5   6

Year of CEO's tenure

1. Prior CEO Baseline is the average number of M&A transactions closed annually during the previous CEO's tenure
Source: S&P, BoardEx, BCG Henderson Institute analysis

Figure 1.4: Successful CEOs gain license from early M&A to accelerate deal activity.

Ronnie Leten, one such example, led Atlas Copco, the Nordics' largest industrials firm, from 2009 to 2017. In his first letter to shareholders,[8] Leten outlined a growth strategy whereby Atlas Copco would achieve one-third of its future growth through acquisitions. In his first 18 months, Leten maintained a similar deal cadence as his predecessor, acquiring nine firms with Kr1.4 billion in sales in total at the time of acquisition. Then he dramatically accelerated M&A, acquiring three dozen firms with Kr12 billion in sales over the next four years. The company's market capitalization quadrupled over his eight-year tenure as CEO.

---

8 https://www.atlascopcogroup.com/content/dam/atlas-copco/corporate/documents/invest ors/financial-publications/english-archive/Annual%20Report%20incl.%20Sustainability% 20Report%20and%20Corporate%20Governance%20Report%202009.pdf.

3. They emphasize non-financial, in addition to financial, performance.
In line with the increased focus by investors and other stakeholders on non-financial performance, over the last 15 years the average company has been improving ESG performance. However, we find that successful CEOs are increasing their companies' ESG scores at twice the rate of bottom-quintile CEOs. This may be a byproduct of overall competence, as underperforming CEOs may not have as much bandwidth to focus on non-financial factors, or it could be that focus on ESG is a driver of sustained outperformance in its own right, since doing well on important social issues is good for sustainable value generation[9] in the long run. By whichever mechanism, the best CEOs create not only good fundamentals and stock price performance, but also create a lasting legacy.[10]

Breaking ESG down into its components, the best performing CEOs did especially well on governance – perhaps not surprising given the unique role that CEOs play in setting the organizational model. Specifically, in alignment with recent increased interest in multi-stakeholder governance models, they improve CSR (corporate social responsibility) strategy and management scores, focusing less singularly on shareholder-related issues.

John Chambers, CEO of Cisco from 1995 to 2015, is one such example. As CEO, Chambers increased the company's market capitalization from $8B to over $144B while remaining deeply committed to creating social value. During his tenure, Cisco founded the *Networking Academy*, an IT skills and career-building program aimed at teaching students the skills required to design, build, manage, and secure networks. In 2017, the program celebrated its 20th anniversary, boasting 7.8 million students in 180 countries.

4. They pay more attention to diversity. A more diverse workforce generates a wider range of ideas, and therefore more innovation potential[11] – which is especially necessary in a business environment in which competitive advantage has become less persistent.[12]

For CEOs that take over large companies, it is difficult to make instant progress in changing the composition of entire organizations. However, a leading indicator of progress on diversity is the composition of *new hires* under a CEO's tenure. Although gender parity remains elusive even in the most diverse firms, top-performing CEOs increase the percentage of women new hires (from 36% to 38%), while bottom-quintile CEOs oversee a slight decline (from 31% to 30%). Gender

---

9 https://www.bcg.com/en-us/publications/2019/optimize-social-business-value.
10 https://www.bcg.com/en-us/publications/2018/algorithm-successful-21st-century-ceo.
11 https://www.bcg.com/publications/2019/winning-the-20s-business-imperative-of-diversity.
12 https://sloanreview.mit.edu/article/fighting-the-gravity-of-average-performance/.

diversity is only one of many dimensions of diversity that matters, of course, but it is the one for which data is mostly widely available and we hypothesize that top performing CEOs pay more attention to diversity more broadly.

Success Factors in Specific Contexts

While a handful of factors align with strong CEO performance across all contexts, the impact of other strategic moves varies by context.

On average, 27% of senior executives exit by the end of the first year under a new CEO. Not surprisingly, from a weak company starting position (characterized by two-year trailing TSR underperformance of 20 percentage points or more), early executive turnover rates rise to 33%.

CEOs that turn a weak company starting position into a top-quintile CEO tenure have the highest rate of turnover, seeing 38% of executives exit by the end of their first year. In contrast, there is no difference in turnover between successful and unsuccessful CEOs that inherit a strong starting position (see Figure 1.5).

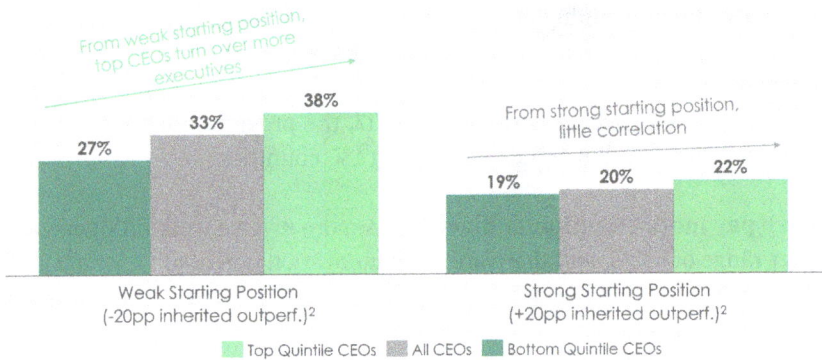

1. Percentage of executives remaining after Year 1 from pool of executives in the year before start of CEO tenure
2. Starting position defined as trailing 2y average outperformance prior to start of CEO tenure
Source: Thomson Reuters, S&P, BoardEx, BCG Henderson Institute analysis

Figure 1.5: Executive turnover in first year of CEO tenure.

Corporate transformations represent yet another avenue for new CEOs to leave their mark. Our research shows that transformation is difficult and that the majority of such initiatives fail to create value – in large part because most companies, rather than changing preemptively, wait until they have no choice but to do so, and as a result lack the time and freedom needed to pursue longer term moves.

When corporate transformation is necessary, those that recognize the need for change early in their tenure and act swiftly tend to have more success than those who wait. Among CEOs who launched transformations during their tenure, those that did so in the first or second year outperformed those who waited longer by 3 percentage points annually. (This is consistent with earlier evidence[13] that having fresh leadership improves the odds of a successful change effort.)

A CEO's Personal Characteristics

We may have a stereotypical image of a successful leader. In most instances, however, the demographic background of a CEO tends to have no observed impact on the odds of success. For example, we observe no significant difference in CEO impact as a result of gender. However, one variable where differences do arise is the hiring route. CEOs hired externally tend to perform no better or worse than those hired internally on average, but they do have a wider *spread* of outcomes – both on the upside and the downside.

Beyond demographic factors, it is plausible that the personality traits of CEOs might influence success. Motivated by recent research that demonstrated that Big Five personality scores can be reliably inferred from CEOs' language when discussing their companies, we used machine learning to infer the traits of CEOs from responses given during the Q&A portion of quarterly earnings calls.[14]

We found that, overall, CEOs of all personality types could be successful, and on almost all dimensions there was little gap between the best- and worst-performing leaders. Put another way, we found no personality profile which either guaranteed or precluded success.

However, there was one area with some difference: underperforming CEOs were more likely to score highly on the "Conscientiousness" dimension. While this personality trait implies reliability and diligence, it also connotes a preference for goal-directed planning, which comes at the expense of spontaneity, adaptability,

---

13 https://sloanreview.mit.edu/article/the-truth-about-corporate-transformation/.
14 Harrison et al. (April 2019). Measuring CEO Personality: Developing, validating, and testing a linguistic tool. *Strategic Management Journal*.

and agility.[15] While such a profile may be powerful in more junior positions, in to-day's complex and dynamic business environment, it is perhaps less suitable for success at the highest levels. We have shown elsewhere that, in recent dec-ades, classical strategic planning is no longer a panacea[16] and needs to be supplemented by more dynamic approaches to strategy, as technology and other factors accelerate the rate of business model evolution and erode the durability of competitive advantage. De-averaging by industry, this pattern is most pronounced in tech-intensive and dynamic industries (IT, Communica-tions, Consumer Discretionary).

Implications

While every CEO tenure is different, our findings suggest that there is a pattern of moves and characteristics that tend to improve the odds of being successful. Together, they point to a larger set of principles that CEOs can learn from:

1. Strive to defy the average. Though the magnitude of the CEO effect can be greater in some contexts and lower in others, there is a significant gap between the top and bottom CEOs in every industry and type of company. This is consis-tent with earlier evidence that the spread of performance between companies in a given industry is much greater than the spread of performance between industries.[17] As a result, leaders should focus less on "best practices" (which tend to level performance), and more on innovation and new opportunities in order to be exceptional and defy the average. Strategy is often conducted with the assumption that sector is a significant determinant of a company's fate, but the evidence would suggest otherwise.

There is significant competitive advantage to be gained even in times of cri-sis. In economic downturns, competitive volatility increases, and 14% of compa-nies increase both revenue growth and margin[18] in absolute terms. Furthermore, the evidence indicates that a long-term, growth-oriented perspective is important

---

15 John, Oliver P., and Sanjay Srivastava (1999). "The Big-Five Trait Taxonomy: History, Mea-surement, and Theoretical Perspectives," *Handbook of personality: Theory and research* (2nd ed.). New York: Guilford. https://pages.uoregon.edu/sanjay/pubs/bigfive.pdf.

16 https://www.amazon.com/Your-Strategy-Needs-Execute-Approach-ebook/dp/B00O92Q6DU.

17 https://www.bcg.com/publications/2019/bad-time-to-be-average.

18 https://www.bcg.com/publications/2019/advantage-in-adversity-winning-next-downturn.

to emerging from a downturn stronger. Amid the current crisis, leaders should not focus only on weathering the storm, but also on taking advantage of new opportunities and reimagining their businesses for the future.[19] In other words, a downturn is a better opportunity for creating competitive advantage than more stable times.

2. Identify key moves and act preemptively. A common theme among successful CEOs is that they took early action where necessary – they accelerated turnover of underperforming management teams, they weren't hesitant to make deals early in their tenure, and they embarked upon transforming their organizations early when needed.

Even for long-tenured CEOs, there is value in preemptively initiating change.[20] But whereas new leaders often come in with a fresh perspective and a burning platform, incumbent leaders need to fight harder to avoid complacency or inertia, in order to recognize new threats and mobilize against them.

3. Take a de-averaged and dynamic approach to strategy. Traditionally, the role of corporate leaders has often been to set clear goals and define unchanging plans to achieve them. However, in an increasingly uncertain and fast-moving context, classical planning processes are not always the best approach. Accordingly, leaders that are overly "goal-oriented" have tended to perform worse, especially in disrupted industries. Instead, the most successful leaders are more likely to adopt the right approach to strategy in each part of the business,[21] and in particular to use dynamic and/or creative approaches where necessary.

4. Articulate and fulfill a positive social purpose. Increasingly, top CEOs are being called on to serve a broader range of stakeholders than shareholders alone, and in the long run businesses must create value for society to continue to attract talent, customers, and capital. The most successful CEOs attend to these issues by articulating a purpose beyond maximizing financial returns and by improving performance on non-financial dimensions too. The expectations of the social contributions of corporations are increasing and leaders will in-

---

19 https://www.bcg.com/publications/2020/business-resilience-lessons-covid-19.
20 https://www.bcg.com/publications/2018/preemptive-transformation-fix-it-before-it-breaks.
21 https://www.amazon.com/Your-Strategy-Needs-Execute-Approach-ebook/dp/B00O92Q6DU.

creasingly need to pursue sustainable business model innovation[22] to co-optimize for business and societal benefits.

CEOs are in the spotlight more than ever as they lead their companies through the current crisis. By understanding principles underpinning when and how much leadership matters, and factors that increase the odds of success, leaders can learn valuable lessons about navigating today's challenges.

---

22 https://www.bcg.com/en-us/publications/2020/quest-sustainable-business-model-innovation.

Martin Reeves, Sandy Moose, Kevin Whitaker

Chapter 2
The Board's Role in Strategy in a Changing Environment

As change in the business environment accelerates, it requires the same of not just businesses but also their boards of directors. Given the increased variety of business environments and the growing importance of non-competitive forces, corporate strategy is increasingly complex – and an increasingly important driver of performance. Furthermore, directors are facing increased calls from other stakeholders, including management and investors, to be more deeply involved in setting strategy.

However, the current reality is that the extent and manner of engagement in strategy still varies widely from board to board. What benefits can directors bring to the table, and what are the best practices of forward-looking companies when it comes to the board's role in strategy?

Strategy is Increasingly Important

Corporate strategy is increasingly challenging for today's leaders. Business environments are becoming more and more varied, which requires companies to actively choose strategic approaches that match their own specific situations.[1] External forces such as political pressures, social expectations, and macroeconomic circumstances are having greater impacts, adding to the complexity of strategy. And the increasing pace of change means that strategic assumptions must be re-evaluated constantly.

At the same time, corporate strategy is also becoming more important. With aggregate growth trending downward globally and new competitors presenting a constant threat of disruption, companies can no longer count on merely extending and exploiting historical strategies over the long term. This means that strategy has become a more important source of differentiation between firms: Within a given industry, the average dispersion of performance has doubled since the 1980s (see Figure 2.1).

---

[1] https://store.hbr.org/product/your-strategy-needs-a-strategy-how-to-choose-and-execute-the-right-approach/14054?sku=14054-HBK-ENG.

https://doi.org/10.1515/9783110775174-002

STANDARD DEVIATION OF ECONOMIC PROFIT (%)[1]

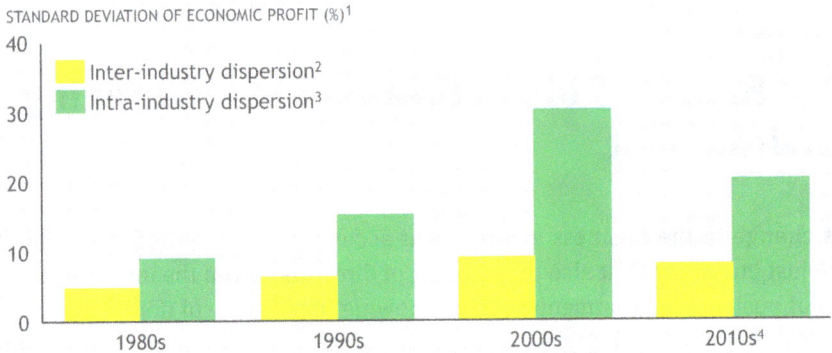

Sources: S&P Capital IQ; BCG Henderson Institute analysis.
[1]Economic profit (%) = Return on equity (%) - Cost of capital (%). For simplification, cost of capital is assimilated to average risk-free rate of capital over the decade.
[2]Industries are based on the GICS classification (N=68). Includes all US-listed companies with average total common equity >$50 million over each decade (N=6,526).
[3]Average of intra-industry dispersion for the 68 industries from GICS classifications. [4]2010-2016.

Figure 2.1: Spread of performance within industries has exploded.

Given the growing importance and complexity of strategy, other stakeholders are demanding that directors focus more on the topic. For example, the leaders of Vanguard, Blackrock, and State Street (the three largest shareholders of U.S. corporations) have all publicly called for boards to be deeply involved in setting strategy within the last year.[2]

In the past, shareholder activism has generally been associated with financial engineering and other actions with an immediate payoff. However, passive investors – those with long-term holdings who do not benefit from any short-term value creation that is not sustained – account for an increasing share of ownership. This suggests that we should expect an increase in a new type of shareholder activism, focused on corporate strategy and issues with long-term impact. (Indeed, a majority of institutional investors already say the most important factor in supporting activist campaigns is a "credible story

---

2 Vanguard Chairman William McNabb's key questions for CEOs for the Strategic Investor Initiative (February 2018), https://cif.cecp.co/; Blackrock CEO Larry Fink's open letter to CEOs (January 2018), https://www.blackrock.com/corporate/investor-relations/larry-fink-ceo-letter; State Street Global Advisors CEO Ronald O'Hanley in interview (October 2017), https://www.fcltglobal.org/resource/an-interview-with-ronald-ohanley-president-and-chief-executive-offi cer-of-ssga/.

focusing on long-term strategy."[3]) Accordingly, directors must make sure they are attending to strategic issues responsibly.

Similar demands are not limited to investors: Nearly all CEOs also say that their boards should spend more time on strategy.[4] Based on the business environment and the beliefs of other stakeholders, board members have a clear mandate to become more involved in strategy. So why is this often challenging in practice?

Board Involvement is Challenging, But Can Add Substantial Value

At first glance, it sounds like a trivial observation that boards should be highly involved in corporate strategy. Directors themselves recognize the need: Collectively, they rate long-term strategic planning as the top issue demanding attention by the board.[5]

The fact is, however, many boards are ill-equipped to deal with strategy in the modern environment. They may not have the appropriate expertise: Many directors at incumbent companies built their careers in a "classical" business environment and may not have proven capabilities to master the variety of strategic approaches that are required today.

Furthermore, directors typically have many different roles and competing commitments, limiting their available time and energy. Their legal mandates center on topics like audit, compensation, and governance. Regulatory obligations, such as those prescribed in the Sarbanes-Oxley Act, have increased directors' focus on compliance. And new risks, including cybersecurity, data privacy, and harassment, are drawing more attention from boards. These demands can collectively crowd out directors' attention to strategy.

As a result, there is wide variation in board engagement on strategy. On one end of the spectrum, some may lean toward a less active role: For example, in a recent survey more than half of directors said that management, rather than the board of directors, is responsible for identifying potential strategic

---

3 "Institutional Investor Survey 2018," Morrow Sodali, https://morrowsodali.com/uploads/articles/attachments/1540899113-investor-survey-june-2018.pdf.
4 https://www.bcg.com/publications/2016/strategy-value-creation-strategy-how-nordic-boards-create-exceptional-value.
5 NYSE/SpencerStuart, "What Directors Think" (2016), https://www.nyse.com/publicdocs/WDT_Report_2016.pdf.

disruptions at their company.[6] Yet at the other end of the spectrum, some boards have a very hands-on approach: In the same survey, a small minority said they have a separate board committee that studies disruption risk.

Boards can add significant value by focusing on challenging and shaping strategy in a number of ways:

Focusing on the Long Run to Complement Management

Management often has a tendency to focus on the short-term picture. This is understandable – and necessary – given that running the business presents constant challenges. (CEOs themselves recognize this tendency: 86% say they focus more on the short term than the long term.[7]) But for the firm to remain vital over time, it must also pay attention to the future. By sitting outside the day-to-day operations, directors are in an ideal position to counter-balance management's tendencies and focus on the long run – enabling the firm to act strategically on multiple timescales.

Leveraging Embeddedness

The impact of external forces on business is increasing. Reflecting this, our research shows that companies discuss political and economic factors more frequently than ever[8] in their annual reports. Board members can uniquely use their external connections to understand the broader picture and use it to help build a resilient firm. By leveraging their different backgrounds, as well as their connections to other stakeholders through concurrent involvement in different businesses or industries, directors may be able to detect emerging threats or opportunities more quickly and ensure that the firm responds accordingly.

---

6 NYSE/SpencerStuart, "What Directors Think" (2017), http://boardmember.com/wp-content/uploads/2017/10/WDT_Report_2017-1.pdf.
7 CECP Board of Boards, "Executive Report: Competing for the Long Run" (2016), http://cecp.co/wp-content/uploads/2016/11/BofB16_Executive_Summary_FINAL_Web.pdf.
8 https://www.bcg.com/publications/2017/corporate-strategy-business-no-longer.

Contributing Cross-Domain Insights

As industry boundaries are blurred by new technologies and business models, sector-specific knowledge is no longer sufficient. Given the risk of digital disruption, leadership must be informed about emerging technologies and new competitors. When selected thoughtfully, directors can fill gaps in management's skills or knowledge in key areas.

Governing Firm Strategy and Execution

Given the increased stakes and complexity of strategy, its governance is more and more important. Boards are in a unique position to pressure-test management's decision-making, ensuring that the strategy is tailored to each business environment and continually probing key assumptions to make sure they remain valid. Furthermore, directors can use their role to monitor the execution of strategy to ensure it is being carried out properly.

Together, these actions transform the board's engagement model for strategy well beyond a "rubber stamp." Instead, boards should take an "activist" approach and think about how to challenge and disrupt their own strategy – before an actual activist (or competitor) does so.

Strategic Focus Requires a New Board Model

As the strategic demands of directors evolve, so do their required skills. A board that is drawn from a homogeneous industry or financial background will leave some strategic benefits on the table. Where possible, firms should aim to select directors with a variety of relevant skills, which may include technological knowledge or political expertise.

At the same time, boards must balance the risk of becoming too bloated, and therefore unable to effectively make decisions and provide governance. According to our research of large US firms,[9] companies with larger boards have lower average growth over the following five years even when controlling for relevant factors such as company size and age. This relationship is not limited to any one industry in particular (e.g., tech companies), and it is statistically significant and predictive of future growth.

---

9 https://fortune.com/future-50/.

Therefore, boards should not attempt to check off every possible box of expertise, especially in emerging areas such as cybersecurity, where finding directors with legitimate skills is very difficult. Instead, management and the board should regularly seek advice from independent experts who are more up to date with new developments in these fields. This way, leadership can recognize and address any gaps in its thinking – perhaps in the form of information on new technologies, or perhaps through a different viewpoint on the firm's strategy as a whole. For instance, directors might ask a successful tech entrepreneur, "How would you disrupt our company?"

Best Practices of Highly Involved Boards

How can companies build boards that are capable of effectively shaping strategy?

1. Board meetings feature a range of ideas and viewpoints. Directors themselves should represent a diversity of perspectives to improve the group's collective decision-making. Gender and ethnic diversity certainly help in this regard, but they are not enough: Additional sources of heterogeneity – such as age, industry or educational specialties, and international experience – also increase the potential range of innovative ideas.[10]

Diversity may be an obvious goal, but is often elusive in practice. A recent study indicates that directors with similar backgrounds (male, financial experience, served on other boards) remain overrepresented today, with negative impacts on firm performance.[11] This does not mean that companies should try to "check every box" of representation, which risks a bloated and ineffective board. However, they should ensure that a variety of viewpoints and backgrounds are always represented.

Board meetings should regularly involve external experts, adding fresh perspectives that can be tailored to the most pressing issues. To ensure that outside voices are integrated into the strategic process, directors should also be chosen for their ability to engage in productive debate – for example, being

---

[10] https://hbr.org/2018/01/how-and-where-diversity-drives-financial-performance.

[11] Erel, Isil, Léa H. Stern, Chenhao Tan, and Michael S. Weisbach (2018), "Research: Could Machine Learning Help Companies Select Better Board Directors?" *Harvard Business Review*, April 9, 2018, https://hbr.org/2018/04/research-could-machine-learning-help-companies-select-better-board-directors.

receptive to new views, challenging others' ideas in a constructive manner, and being motivated to engage in strategy deeply and collectively.

2. The board challenges management adeptly – and management is receptive to challenge. No matter how capable the executive team is, an external perspective can always help ensure the strategy is more robust. However, board members may have difficulty asking the tough questions – perhaps because they do not know what or how to probe due to information asymmetry. Or perhaps because they do not want to appear disruptive. (This is a long-standing problem: As Warren Buffett wrote thirty years ago, "At board meetings, criticism of the CEO's performance is often viewed as the social equivalent of belching."[12]) And some CEOs are less receptive to challenges, perceiving tough questions as hostile.

To avoid these pitfalls, directors must act as "loyal critics," mastering the art of challenging management while preserving trust. This starts by building a working relationship outside of formal meetings, so directors know what issues to focus on and the CEO is prepared to engage productively in the process. Then the board should ask challenging questions – ones that make critical hidden details explicit by foregrounding strategic assumptions and essential features of the broader context.

Examples of probing questions include:
- What are plausible scenarios for the future of our industry?
- Will our strategy be robust to changes in the macro environment?
- What are the sensitivities of key assumptions?
- How do you ensure adequate implementation of the strategy?
- Do we have the right talent to execute it, for now and the future?
- What are the potential downside risks and mitigation plans?

The board and management should iterate until these questions are answered with sufficient clarity and precision. To ensure every decision receives thorough scrutiny, directors might institute a rule of "compulsory dissent": No strategy may be endorsed until at least one robust counterproposal has been explicitly offered and considered.

3. Directors monitor execution of the strategy. Execution cannot be separated from strategy – they are intertwined.[13] Just as the approach to strategy should be modulated according to the environment, so too should the approach to execution.

---

12 1988 Berkshire Hathaway Annual Report.
13 https://hbr.org/2017/11/your-strategy-has-to-be-flexible-but-so-does-your-execution.

The board can play a vital role in ensuring that strategy is implemented through-out the organization, but it can be difficult in practice: According to a National Association of Corporate Directors survey, 67% of directors say it is important to improve their monitoring of strategy execution.

Effectively monitoring strategy execution is not as simple as watching a dashboard of results. The board should make sure that management is evaluated on both financial and non-financial dimensions, with a clear prioritization of metrics in line with the firm's overall goals. This avoids the pitfalls of an exces-sively long list of measurements, in which a few good ones can be highlighted while others are explained away or overlooked.

Additionally, directors should meet with management frequently to test that the original assumptions behind the strategy still hold. Follow-up meetings should involve not only the CEO but other layers of management, ensuring that strategy is being implemented throughout the entire organization. These can be complemented by employee surveys to understand the execution in even more detail. For example, during a large transformation, the board might identify where in the organization employees do not understand the strategy, do not see progress in the change effort, or do not believe they have sufficient resour-ces to implement it.

4. Boards dedicate more time to strategy and keep discussions focused.
Given directors' other responsibilities and the infrequent nature of board meet-ings, it is challenging for them to stay up to date on key trends and continu-ously validate the firm's strategic direction. Though directors say they want to spend more time on strategy, the reality is that instead they are increasing their time spent on other topics,[14] such as governance and risk.

To ensure sufficient focus on strategic topics, boards should schedule dedi-cated time to discuss strategy in the agenda of every board meeting – not only on an annual cycle. Furthermore, a robust knowledge system can give directors the information they need: Frequent updates should keep directors apprised of changes in the environment and resulting impacts on firm strategy. Extensive communication before and after board meetings can streamline the sessions themselves, freeing up time for strategic discussion. And directors should have access to a repository of on-demand materials to increase their inside knowl-edge of the company.

Time and information alone are not sufficient, however: Even when time has been carved out for strategy, the discussion often devolves quickly to more

---

14 https://www.bcg.com/publications/2016/people-organization-leadership-talent-looking-smoke-under-door.

familiar territory, such as granular details or the firm's current operations. For example, if the board intends to discuss marketing strategy, it may soon find itself focusing on sales strategies instead, and eventually questioning the firm's practices in managing a sales force. These discussions may yield useful suggestions, but by ignoring the bigger picture, they represent a missed opportunity for the board to add even more value. The best board chairs can keep discussion focused on key strategic issues – a very difficult task, but one that is crucial.

A changing business environment calls for an enhanced role of directors in relation to strategy. Strategy is becoming more challenging yet more important, increasing the value of boards that can actively partner with management and guide the company's future direction. By practicing "self-activism" – challenging assumptions, offering counterarguments, and closely monitoring execution – boards can help develop a strategy to succeed in the modern age.

Diana Dosik, Vikram Bhalla, Allison Bailey
Chapter 3
A Lot Will Change – So Must Leadership

Before the coronavirus struck, it was already clear that winning the '20s would require approaches to business fundamentally different from those of the past. Becoming a bionic company[1] – one that unleashes the full potential of people *and* technology – was already becoming an imperative. The COVID-19 pandemic seems only to have accelerated the need for this transformation. In order to survive, thrive, and compete successfully, companies now have just two years (or less) to get to where they might otherwise have hoped to be in five.

Among the many pressing demands on leaders, transforming their companies to adopt a new, "bionic" operating model may be the most urgent and will require them to lead in new ways. A lot will change in the world and so must they.

What do leaders really *need* to do – what really needs to change – as they transform their companies to become bionic in the post-COVID world? We see four imperatives: (1) Leaders must rethink the art of the possible, (2) they must move from managing to enabling, (3) they must harness the full power of technology, and (4) they must translate purpose into action (see Figure 3.1).

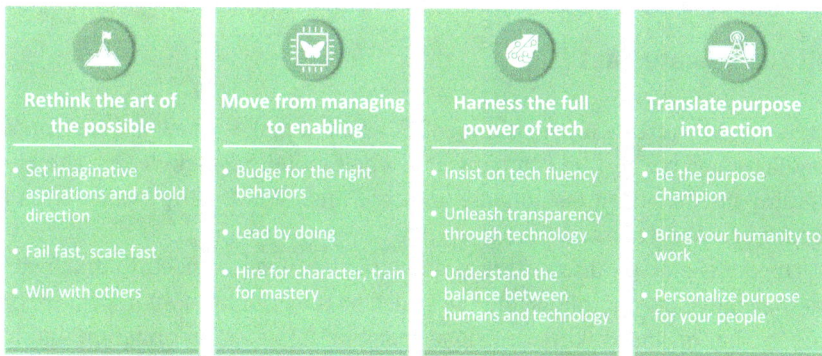

Rethink the art of the possible	Move from managing to enabling	Harness the full power of tech	Translate purpose into action
• Set imaginative aspirations and a bold direction	• Budge for the right behaviors	• Insist on tech fluency	• Be the purpose champion
• Fail fast, scale fast	• Lead by doing	• Unleash transparency through technology	• Bring your humanity to work
• Win with others	• Hire for character, train for mastery	• Understand the balance between humans and technology	• Personalize purpose for your people

Source: BCG analysis.

Figure 3.1: Imperatives for the leaders of bionic companies.

---

[1] https://www.bcg.com/capabilities/digital-technology-data/bionic-company.

https://doi.org/10.1515/9783110775174-003

Rethink the Art of the Possible

Technology creates new possibilities. With the exponential changes that surround us, it is imperative for a company to embrace these new possibilities, not just as a cost lever but as a means of breaking compromises. It is critical that leaders direct their teams to really reimagine the future.

Set an Imaginative Aspiration and Bold Direction

To develop a truly bionic company, leaders must envision new and ambitious operating models with technology at the core. That means reimagining how work gets done and what gets delivered. Netflix was a very early example of this, envisioning a digital future for entertainment (that the rest of the industry scoffed at, and that some companies eventually paid a steep price for dismissing) and then setting a bold course toward that goal.

Similarly, bionic companies start from tomorrow and work backward, not from today forward. One of the CEOs we know said, "It's not about tech replacing people. My job and that of my leadership team is to think of new questions and new problems that we can now solve with people and tech together. That is the game. That is my job."

Fail Fast, Scale Fast

Leaders need to create an environment in which it makes sense not just for individual teams but for the company as a whole to fail fast and learn. The idea of failing fast has been fashionable for some time. What many leaders miss is the idea of scaling fast.

Once ideas or products start to gain traction, leaders need to make sure that they move beyond pilots and are scaled so they can have an impact on the market. That means making decisions based on imperfect information and investing boldly, taking a portfolio approach on a few significant bets. Amazon has codified this bias toward action in one of its leadership principles – "We value calculated risk taking" – amply illustrated by the success of one-day shipping through Prime and Amazon Web Services.

Win With Others

Business is often conceived as a zero-sum war between competitors, but for bionic companies it is much more valuable to focus on finding win-win scenarios and opportunities for reciprocity. Understand not only what your company can deliver to customers, but what it could deliver to other members of an ecosystem as a partner, supplier, source of talent, or convener. In some cases, even direct competitors can create such arrangements, as North Face and Patagonia have done in their shared bid to promote conservation. One CEO put it this way: "It is incumbent on me to have a view to lift my whole industry and all our partners. I can't win in a barren desert."

Move from Managing to Enabling

In a bionic company, where technology performs many routine tasks, the most important human contributions will be creativity, cooperation, ethical and business judgment, and an understanding of context. In order for employees to bring these skills and contributions to their work, they will need to be engaged very differently. It won't be enough to just direct them to perform the narrow tasks in their job descriptions. Leaders must work to enable their people to bring their full potential to the job.

Nudge for the Right Behaviors

Culture and behaviors that align with that culture are critical in any company. Often this alignment requires the use of traditional levers like compensation, the allocation of scarce resources, and the selection of people to fill specific roles. But in a bionic company, it also means leveraging technology and behavioral science to strengthen the needed behaviors. Leaders must use real-time reminders, gamification, rapid feedback loops, and other nudge tools at scale to transform culture and individual behaviors and cement desired habits over time.

In India, for example, early-childhood education is often delivered by teachers with very limited formal training or oversight. A government client wanted to make improvements, but retraining teachers or hiring new ones would have been a herculean task requiring significant expense. Instead, the leaders of the effort took the time to understand the behavioral changes that needed to be made. They then had an app designed and installed on each teacher's phone that included simple features such as a calendar of daily activities, videos demonstrating the way each one should be performed, and a point system in which teachers could compete to rise on a shared leaderboard. This use of nudges, gamification, and positive feedback reshaped teacher behavior, increasing the time spent on learning activities by 60%, with 74% of teachers logging on daily. As one leader put it, "We helped them exactly where they needed it – in the classroom."

Lead by Doing

The idea that "leaders lead, managers review, doers do" no longer applies in a bionic company. Leaders need to be involved with the teams driving innovation and with the people interacting with customers so that they can play a first-hand role in shaping and accelerating the change journey.

In one health care company, senior leaders stopped holding their traditional monthly reviews. Instead, they started visiting team rooms, sitting in on morning meetings, and talking directly with customers – which energized the staff and significantly reduced communication overhead. As the CEO told us, "I don't wait for the review where it's backward looking. I get out there with the team so I can share my vision where the work is happening."

Hire for Character, Train for Mastery

In a bionic company, it's especially important to hire for the intangibles: integrity, good judgment, creativity, and entrepreneurialism. "Apart from some core skills, I look for the integrators, the disruptors, the innovators, the steadfast deliverers. We need all of them," said the CEO of an insurance company.

At the same time, the bionic company must learn to reskill at scale and build T-shaped skills: a broad base with one deep area of expertise. A leading consumer goods company redefined its career paths so that every step helps build the critical skills needed for future leadership. To accelerate learning, the company ensures that leaders are regularly given new roles in new settings with new teams. It has also partnered with several learning providers and curated a learning offer for leaders using technology to enable the adequate scale and personalization.

Harness the Full Power of Technology

Leaders of a bionic company need to get beneath the surface of buzzwords like "digital" and "technology," not necessarily as technologists but as navigators and advanced users. They need to know how to make bold decisions and use the power of technology to reshape their leadership models.

Insist on Tech Fluency

At one Asian conglomerate, top leaders working from home during the pandemic were tasked with completing an advanced learning program, delivered by leading academics and practitioners, on technology, geopolitics, and behavioral science. The program was part of a curated leadership learning series delivered entirely remotely. Those particular topics were chosen because leaders need to be able to speak knowledgeably and persuasively about digital technology, AI, behavioral psychology, and cognitive science if they are to leverage experts, bring an interdisciplinary perspective to teams, and refine strategy in response to new developments.

Leaders also need to build credibility through action, which means experimenting with cutting-edge tools and ways of working instead of hewing to older methods because they are more comfortable. Leaders who do this will set a standard for tech fluency that will help the company attract young talent, retain senior experts, and move their companies forward.

Unleash Transparency by Using Technology

Leaders must leverage technology to build systems of information and transparency. When a lot of information is easily available, the bar can be raised on how much teams are expected to use it on a regular basis. For instance, they can use information to course correct more frequently, to identify a broader cohort of people to help find creative solutions to tough problems, and to increase people's confidence that the company is making ethical, data-based decisions.

When a financial institution that wanted to spend less on travel published data on travel expenses by team, it raised expectations regarding people's responsibility to learn from those who had spent less. When another institution published salary levels, issues of pay equity were exposed that the company was then able to address, increasing employee confidence in its commitment to fairness. And when an agricultural company released 12 of its key challenges to an external "crowd" of thinkers, each was solved within a year – including one breakthrough solution from a scientist outside of the agriculture field.

In the past, transparency involved significant cost and needed to be traded off against the work of codifying and disseminating information. That tradeoff has been broken, providing leaders with a significant potential advantage.

Understand the Balance Between Humans and Technology

New technologies hold tremendous promise, but they are not a panacea and they do not function on their own. They have no ethical bounds or common sense, and they can turn small mistakes into colossal collapses owing to their scale and efficiency. Recall, for example, how the failure to notice the implicit biases of AI in recruiting led to a disproportionate focus on stereotyped profiles. It is imperative that leaders retain their responsibility to understand what technology can and cannot do. Leaders need to take advantage of what technology has to offer and complement it with human judgment, so that both are used to their fullest potential.

Translate Purpose into Action

In the transition to the bionic company, purpose matters more than ever. It is the glue that helps integrate all the elements described in this article. As employees grapple with uncertainty and adjust to major change, leaders are called upon to communicate with clarity, to provide continuity, and to empower the organization with a sense of purpose. And they must translate that purpose into action.

Be the Purpose Champion

Leaders must speak loudly and often about why the company exists and why employees should dedicate their professional lives to its success. They give voice to the choices that can and should be made in order to live the company's purpose – such as the uncomfortable tradeoffs[2] involved in valuing quality over speed or environmental friendliness over ease of execution.

---

2 https://www.bcg.com/publications/2019/getting-uncomfortable-on-purpose.

Bring Your Humanity to Work

It's important that leaders leave behind such leadership stereotypes as the "confident decision maker" and the "leader from the front." What employees and others are looking for is an authentic and fully accessible human being. This means sharing much more of yourself – and not just your successes – with many more people. Leaders must engage with their teams and act with compassion and understanding.[3] They must make themselves more visible, available, and accessible through demo days with teams, joint working efforts, and live brainstorming sessions. Several leaders see an opportunity in the current challenges. As one executive explained, "Technology and new ways of working can be an advantage here – leverage technology to have more two-way conversations, more direct outreaches, seeking and acting on feedback from a much larger population than was practical previously."

Personalize Purpose for Your People

Only if purpose is authentic and directly affects employees' roles and teams on a daily basis will they connect to it emotionally and want to live and advocate for it every day. That requires making purpose real through commitments that are tangible, trackable, and felt by employees at work and in their personal lives.

One company that has worked hard in this respect is Unilever, which tracks not only its own progress against purpose but also how connected people feel to that purpose and its impact on their performance. The company's CEO recently revealed that 92% of employees who say that they're able to live their purpose at Unilever also say that they are inspired to go the extra mile for the company.

Becoming a bionic company is a multiyear journey. Especially in the post-COVID world, such companies will be highly advantaged, but they require a new kind of leadership and a significant leap beyond the old paradigms. Fortunately, new beliefs and behaviors are often forged in crisis. Leaders who approach the post-crisis world with an eye toward developing these new attitudes and habits will not only be better able to successfully navigate the immediate aftermath of the pandemic, they will also be better set up for a bionic future.

---

3 https://www.thinkbrighthouse.com/2020/03/leading-with-humanity-and-purpose-in-times-of-crisis/.

Peter Tollman, Martin Reeves
Chapter 4
When Leadership Matters Most

In the midst of the COVID-19 crisis, leaders are doing their best to chart the right course under harsh and unpredictable conditions, knowing that the morale, via- bility, and prosperity of their organizations depend upon them getting this right. Leadership matters most in moments of extreme stress. Most leaders don't have direct experience of leading through a crisis of this magnitude and there is value in synthesizing what we know about the traps and success factors.

Common Traps Across Organizations Today

A number of common traps are in plain sight as we examine organizations today.

1. Invisible Leaders
A crisis will pull leaders into an endless succession of top team meetings where the issues are discussed and strategies determined. While necessary, if this crowds out communications between leaders and employees, it can create un- necessary aimlessness and anxiety.

2. Stiff Communications
Many crises follow an unpredictable course, and leaders may hesitate to be spe- cific in case they are later proven wrong. Furthermore, they may be fearful themselves and try to cover this with a calm gloss. The result is formal, inau- thentic communications, which create rather than reduce distance.

3. Communications Gridlock
Many organizations move from being unengaged early in a crisis to becoming hyperactively engaged. An ever-expanding echo chamber develops as everyone emails everyone about various aspects of the crisis, and crisis communications and daily crisis meetings absorb people's time. The main work of the organiza- tion becomes talking about the crisis. This not only crowds out the critical *real* work to be done; it creates exhaustion, and generates a fog of information, which impedes the communication of critical messages.

https://doi.org/10.1515/9783110775174-004

4. Overly Tactical Focus

There are lots of urgent matters to be attended to in a crisis. In the COVID-19 crisis these include hygiene policies, work-from-home policies, travel policies, supply chain adjustments, facilities closures, daily updates, and more. While necessary, these are not sufficient. This short-term focus must be complemented by looking ahead and anticipating what comes next to prevent organizations from perpetually being in reactive mode. In the COVID-19 crisis there must be an equal emphasis on Reaction, Rebound, a likely Recession, and on Reimagining the business in a post-crisis world. Many organizations are primarily focused on the first of these.

5. Introversion

A crisis naturally precipitates a defensive psychological stance. Organizations look inward to address their pressing challenges. But crises such as COVID-19 affect customers, suppliers, industry peers, investors, and other stakeholders equally. Turning away from stakeholders in a time of need is a missed opportunity to create collective solutions, to meet new needs and to build trust.

6. Inertia

The COVID-19 virus is characterized by very-high transmissibility. This has created an epidemic which moves faster than most organizations are able to accommodate. We have seen the dire consequences of losing a week or two before taking action in some European countries.

7. Failure of Imagination

The first casualty of a crisis is imagination. But, while responding to a crisis requires getting certain simple things right without over-thinking them, fundamental solutions and adjustments require more creativity.

Guiding Principles During a Crisis

What then are some of the guiding principles leaders need to heed during a crisis?

1. Be Visible, Purposeful and Authentic

Communicate in ways that engage and increase the relevance of your teams and clarify the reasons underlying your communications.

2. Leverage the Principle of "Commander's Intent"

The Prussian general Helmuth Von Moltke pioneered the idea of *Auftragstaktik* (Commander's Intent) to allow the effective functioning of an organization in the fog of war. Rather than peppering the organization with frequently changing and detailed instructions (and allowing others further down the chain to amplify such behaviors), he shared only the key objectives and their rationale, allowing soldiers to employ whatever tactics were necessary to achieve the objectives in each situation they faced. This not only allows the organization to be flexible and adaptive, but reduces time lags and allows a focus on execution rather than internal communications.

3. Use Multiple Clock Speeds

Leaders need to think on multiple timescales by considering the now, the next, and the later. They need to make sure that leadership teams look ahead. And they need to prepare their organization to pivot to the next wave of considerations.

4. Engage Externally

Your customers and stakeholders need you now. The best intelligence in a crisis comes from the crisis itself and you need frequent, fresh, firsthand information to adapt and respond effectively. You need to be able to see the weak signals that spell new threats and opportunities.

5. Cut Through Bureaucracy

Assemble a multi-functional task force that is empowered to make decisions and suspend normal decision protocols which may require multiple sign-offs and consensus building. Be comfortable making decisions on the best available information and changing them if better information becomes available.

6. Keep Imagination Alive

You will need imaginative solutions. There is advantage in adversity. It's no accident that the Chinese word for crisis combines the characters for danger and opportunity. There will be new needs and new opportunities to serve clients now and beyond the crisis. There will be new opportunities for innovation. The world beyond the crisis will not be a reversion to 2019 reality – attitudes, behaviors, and needs will change. A crisis effectively speeds up the clock: bad things come faster, but so do opportunities. Leaders will need to adopt and help their organizations adopt an ambidextrous mind set – defending, protecting, and reacting on the one hand; and creating, innovating, and imagining on the other.

Now is precisely when leadership has the greatest impact. Effective crisis leadership has a multiplicative effect on organizational capability. Every leader will need to modulate their style to help flip organizations from a peace-time mode to a wartime mode as swiftly and effectively as possible.

Martin Reeves, François Candelon, Kevin Whitaker
Chapter 5
Fostering Organizational Stamina

One of the most common questions managers ask about the COVID-19 crisis is, "When will it be over?"[1] The question reflects an understandable fatigue with living under protracted uncertainty and a desire to return to normalcy. But not only are we unlikely to return to the pre-crisis normal,[2] it could also be quite some time until we reach a new steady state and uncertainty abates. It's even possible that there may be no prolonged equilibrium before the next disruption. How, then, can leaders address a rising sentiment of impatience and foster the stamina required for organizations to successfully adapt to new conditions?

A Long Journey

While we can't be sure when the outbreak will be resolved, it seems likely that it could be protracted. Cumulative case numbers are plateauing in many nations, but the epidemic continues to spread in others. Furthermore, the disease may not end with the first cycle; epidemiologists warn that the disease could exhibit a second wave, as many viral outbreaks have historically had, or could even become endemic, like the seasonal flu. Uncertainty about the disease is likely to persist until at least the widespread deployment of a vaccine, which is not expected until sometime next year in even the most optimistic scenario.

As a result, uncertainty will persist in our everyday lives. For example, hundreds of epidemiologists recently surveyed by the *New York Times*[3] gave a wide spread of opinions on when they would be comfortable resuming common activities. A majority said it would take anywhere from 3–12 months before they

---

1 This article was written in June of 2020, relatively early in the COVID-19 pandemic. While the data and timelines leaders predicted now look optimistic, they provide even further evidence for organizational stamina, as the most successful companies have maintained pace during a pandemic now in its third year.
2 https://www.bcg.com/publications/2020/8-ways-companies-can-shape-reality-post-covid-19.
3 https://www.nytimes.com/interactive/2020/06/08/upshot/when-epidemiologists-will-do-everyday-things-coronavirus.html?campaign_id=154&emc=edit_cb_20200608&instance_id=19194&nl=coronavirus-briefing&regi_id=97463791&segment_id=30390&te=1&user_id=01d3d86468fc00580d806c73404591f7.

https://doi.org/10.1515/9783110775174-005

would feel comfortable going to work in an office or eating at a sit-down restaurant, and most said it would be more than a year before they would attend a sporting event or performance.

Economic uncertainty is also unlikely to disappear quickly. The National Bureau of Economic Research recently confirmed that the US economy is in recession and the World Bank predicts a 5.2% contraction in global GDP in 2020. Cautious consumers are likely to prolong the period of economic uncertainty and adjustment, and unemployment and bankruptcies could have lasting economic effects.

In addition, both the disease and the recession have had created broader impacts across society, bringing concerns about inequality and justice to the forefront. The recent wave of protests in the US and some other countries will likely also have some lasting impact which shapes both policies and consumer behaviors.

It is not surprising therefore that many businesses are increasingly envisioning a long period of uncertainty. According to our survey of hundreds of companies across countries and sectors, as of March 2020, only 14% of companies expected COVID-19 to affect their business for more than 12 months – but by May 2020 that share had more than tripled to 46%. And whereas in the early months of the crisis, only 20–30% of companies expected to make permanent changes in their supply chains, marketing activities, or sales channels, by that May the share had doubled to 40–60% (see the Figure 5.1).

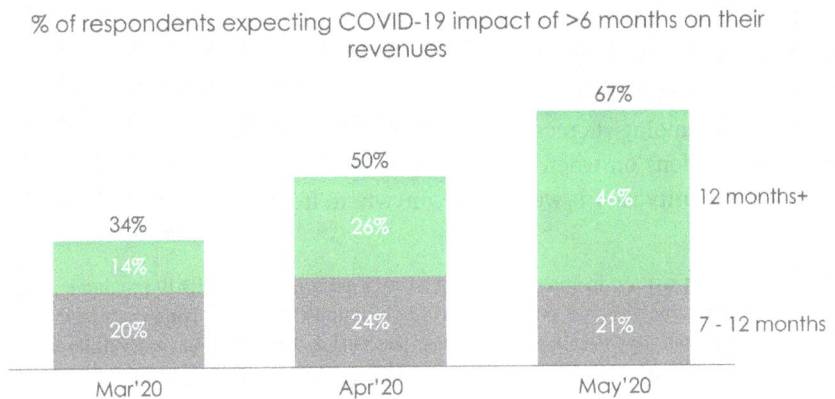

% of respondents expecting COVID-19 impact of >6 months on their revenues

Note: Based on responses received through 21 May
Source: BCG COVID-19 Company Survey; BCG Henderson Institute Analysis

Figure 5.1: Expected duration of COVID-19 impact has increased.

Stamina Pays Off in Crises

Many companies are likely to face challenging, volatile circumstances for the foreseeable future. However, crises also create opportunities for some: our research shows that 10–20% of companies in each sector increase their absolute performance during downturns.[4]

Such "flourishers" demonstrate a very characteristic pattern of behavior. Despite the challenging circumstances, top performers obtain most advantage through differential growth rather than more immediate differential efficiency gains. And they are more likely to take a long-term orientation, focusing not only on day-to-day operational challenges but also on the future of their business. To realize that future, many companies will need to undergo transformation programs that often require significant time and investment. These findings point to a roadmap for success in a crisis that depends not only on the immediate gratification of cost reduction, but on a longer, slower path of growth and reinvention – which requires *organizational stamina*.

Yet prolonged crises like COVID-19 can easily cause individuals to lose stamina and dilute the initial zeal and engagement a crisis can mobilize. This can occur in a number of ways:

1. Loss of energy. The early stages of the outbreak were characterized in many companies by hyperactivity: Newly formed crisis response teams met daily, contingency plans were developed and executed, and frequency of communication accelerated dramatically – all on top of the company's existing operations. These activities were necessary to adapt to rapidly unfolding events, but when the crisis did not disappear but instead became a semi-permanent fixture, individuals continuing to deal with the new uncertainties risk burning out and losing energy.

2. Loss of novelty. Our brains are wired to attend to novel or unexpected phenomena, and after several months of COVID-19 redefining so much of our business and personal activities, the novelty has worn off. Even though the crisis continues to pose significant challenges to companies, employees risk losing attention and becoming distracted. Strange that it may sound, it is entirely possible to become bored with a crisis, even one with fatal consequences.

---

4 https://hbr.org/2019/04/companies-need-to-prepare-for-the-next-economic-downturn.

3. Loss of belief. Persevering against an ongoing challenge requires a conviction that the goal is achievable and your efforts are creating movement toward it. During the depths of a crisis, individuals may lose motivation if they don't see tangible progress resulting from their work. In some industries and companies, rebound may come slowly, and employees can lose hope.

4. Loss of focus. The health and economic effects of the crisis have likely affected everyone in some way, and the stress of continued uncertainty about the future will continue weighing on people for the foreseeable future. Initially this may have been offset by increased adrenaline, but as that fades and the crisis persists, focusing on the task at hand becomes more challenging.

The Recipe for Stamina

How then can leaders build stamina in the face of fatigue brought about by protracted stress and uncertainty? From our research on attaining advantage in adversity and from our observations during the current unfolding crisis, we suggest six factors:

1. Communicate a credible vision. In times of crisis, employees increasingly turn to leaders[5] for guidance and direction. While many tactical matters have to be communicated, such as reopening plans, hygiene policies, and business updates, leaders should not let those crowd out the bigger picture. Articulating a renewed vision of success for the company, and a path to achieving it, will help workers stay engaged.

2. Build confidence with early gains and leading indicators. Once they have a compelling goal, employees will need to see that their efforts are creating progress toward achieving it. In challenging economic circumstances, this will not always show up immediately in traditional financial metrics, which are inherently backward-looking. Instead, leaders need to measure the leading indicators that are directly relevant to the change agenda – and thus increase the visibility of the progress being made.

---

5 https://bcghendersoninstitute.com/when-leadership-matters-most-9ec28db5661f.

3. Set a sustainable pace. We know that speed of decision-making and action matters – transformation programs taken earlier achieve better results.[6] However, persistent change and uncertainty can cause a feeling that there is always more that can be done – and trying to manage too many variables risks burning out staff and managers. Leaders need to identify the real priorities and remove unnecessary or duplicative work in order to keep the organization in it for the long haul. Ultimately this depends on identifying new growth drivers and definitively shifting resources and attention to support their success, rather than supporting too many initiatives.

4. Evolve the focus of efforts over time. The COVID-19 crisis has presented challenges on multiple timescales,[7] from reacting to the initial outbreak and shutdowns, to preparing for possible rebound, to preparing for the recession and recovery, to reimagining the business for the longer run. By shifting the focus to different challenges over time, companies can keep the task at hand fresh and avoid getting stuck in a rut. Furthermore, these different challenges require different types of problem-solving approaches, again arguing for a shifting, multi-phased approach rather than a long slog.

5. Reorient toward growth and innovation. While often necessary, cost-cutting and crisis management are rarely inspiring – and in the long run, a company's performance is driven to a much greater degree by growth and reinvention. By orienting the challenge toward exploiting new possibilities, leaders can unlock employees' imaginations[8] and foster a sense of optimism and control in shaping what will happen next.

6. Show empathy and maintain cohesion. In times of personal uncertainty and social instability, all employees need to know that they are supported and they need to feel part of the collective effort, in spite of geographic remoteness and increased stress in their personal lives. Especially now, leaders need to be authentic and visible – going beyond stiff, formal statements and instead speaking personally and honestly, in ways that create credibility, trust, and affiliation.

---

6 https://www.bcg.com/publications/2018/preemptive-transformation-fix-it-before-it-breaks.
7 https://bcghendersoninstitute.com/fractal-strategy-2ce6898e9f13.
8 https://hbr.org/2020/04/we-need-imagination-now-more-than-ever?ab=hero-main-text.

COVID-19 and its effects will be with us longer than we wish – it won't soon "all be over." The companies that emerge strongest are likely to frame it as an enduring challenge and address it accordingly. By helping preserve energy, novelty, motivation, and peace of mind, leaders can build the stamina in their organizations to see that process through. For those companies, a war of attrition will give way to the flourishing of new opportunity.

Part II: **Leadership Lessons**

Stephen Bungay

Chapter 6
Lessons in Leadership from the Great Commanders

When politicians talk about waging war on something, my heart sinks. They usually do it because they want to turn a crisis into a drama in which they can appear center stage and act out the role of tough, heroic leaders. Good judgment gets left behind in the dressing room. So as the rhetoric of waging war on COVID-19 spread around the world, I felt some foreboding.

That said, political and business leaders can in fact learn a great deal from the great commanders of history, if they know what to look for and where to look.

What to look for is how the great commanders handle crisis, the usual state of affairs in war. They do not turn a crisis into a drama – rather the opposite.

As for where to look, a good place to start is on the western bank of the Tennessee river on the morning on April 6, 1862, almost exactly one year into the conflict that was to become the bloodiest war in American history – at the Battle of Shiloh (Figure 6.1).

Survive, Reset, Thrive

At about 8:30 a.m. on that morning, a small man wearing a battered slouch hat and a rough soldier's coat disembarked from a steamboat at a place called Pittsburg Landing, mounted his horse, and began galloping through the dense woodland to find out what was happening to the troops he had assembled there[1]. Their positions extended out westward toward an unprepossessing log meeting-house which served as a church and was known as Shiloh. It was now the headquarters of the division on the far right of his line, commanded by William Tecumseh Sherman.

The small man's name was Ulysses Simpson Grant, the commander of the Union Army of Tennessee. What he found was mayhem.

---

[1] A book with this title by my colleague Rebecca Homkes will be appearing in 2023. It explains in detail how to lead a breakthrough growth strategy in volatile times.

https://doi.org/10.1515/9783110775174-006

He must have felt pretty bad, for it was partly his fault. Having beaten Confederate forces at Fort Henry and Fort Donelson in February, Grant had been pushing south along the Tennessee river in order to take the railroad at Corinth, Mississippi, a vital link for the South. He expected the Confederates there to wait for him to attack them so that they could benefit from their strong defensive positions. At Pittsburg Landing, his raw troops, many only recently recruited, spent their time practicing much-needed musket drills rather than digging defensive entrenchments. Now unexpectedly under attack, they and their open camps were being quickly overrun.

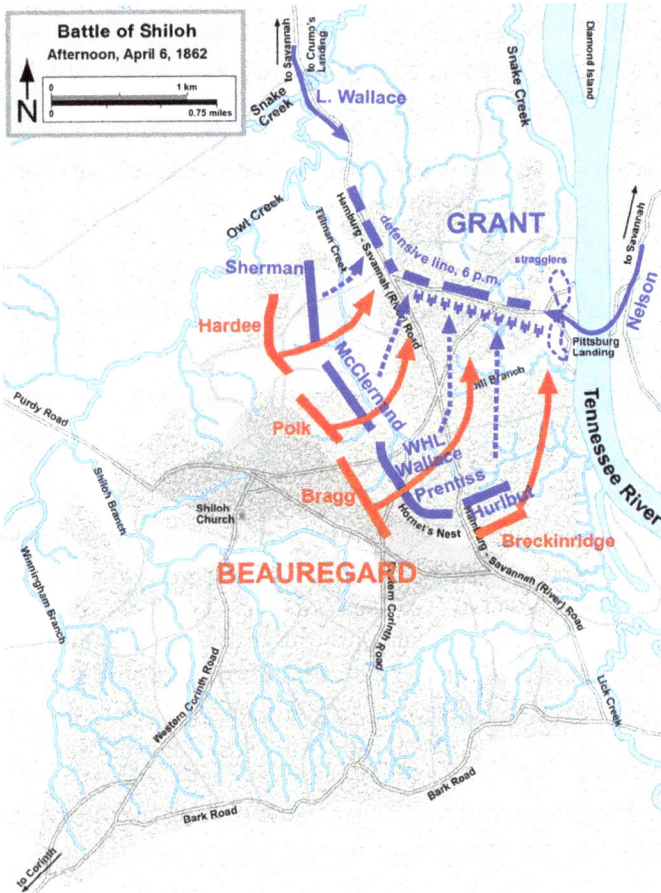

Figure 6.1: The Battle of Shiloh.

Grant visited each of his five divisions in turn. Many of his greenhorn troops were panicking. Just two hours after the main Confederate assault, ammunition was already running short. Actually, there was plenty available, some of it just lying about. Grant gave orders for ammunition to be distributed and told others to do the same. No one else had thought to do so. "The men only wanted someone to give a command," he wrote later.

Regiments were breaking. Some of their Colonels were galloping off in retreat ahead of their men. Where this was happening, Grant stepped in and rallied them. In the center, he encouraged the divisional commanders who were holding on in what became known as "the Hornet's Nest," bringing them reinforcements. As units to the left and right withdrew to shorten Grant's line, the position's exposed flanks made it the epicenter of Confederate attacks. He told his commanders that they must "maintain that position at all hazards." They held on till 5:30 p.m., when they were finally forced to surrender.

But by then, Grant had established a continuous defensive line about a mile back and massed artillery on his left flank by Pittsburg Landing, where he expected the most threatening attack to come. So it did, at around 6:00 p.m., and the artillery concentration of 50 guns beat it back. The fury of the Confederate assault abated and as dusk fell it petered out, just as heavy rain began to fall.

Grant had summoned reinforcements hours earlier. At 8:00 a.m., before getting off his boat, he sent word to his 3rd Division to join him from the north as soon as possible. Once on the field he worried about a bridge over Snake Creek over which he expected them to arrive and another further west over Owl Creek, at the end of Sherman's line, both out of sight to his flank and rear. The 3rd Division was stationed only five miles away, but as dusk fell there was still no sign of them.

At about 9:00 a.m., with chaos and panic around him, Grant had penned a note in the saddle to General Don Carlos Buell, commander of the nearby Army of Ohio, which had been due to join him in his planned push south down the Tennessee River.

He urged Buell to come with all speed to Pittsburg Landing, leaving all his baggage on the east bank. The note was short, perfectly phrased, and without any ambiguity. He told Buell where he would be and that a staff officer would guide him to his place on the field. Buell himself arrived at 1:00 p.m., but by then Grant himself was occupied, personally rallying three regiments in succession as the crisis in the center developed.

The first of Buell's units crossed the Tennessee at about 5:00 p.m. and helped to repulse the final Confederate attack. At midday, the commander of Grant's 3rd Division had started to march his men toward Owl Creek in the west, then learned that the Union line had moved further east, and so countermarched back to the bridge over Snake Creek. They arrived after dark.

The night was quiet.

That evening, Sherman found Grant standing beneath a dripping tree, his coat collar around his ears and a cigar clenched between his teeth. Sherman had sought him out with the intention of advising a retreat. As he spied his face, "some wise and sudden instinct," he later recalled, prompted him otherwise. "Well Grant," he said, "we've had the devil's own day, haven't we?" "Yes," said Grant. "Yes. Lick 'em tomorrow though."

So they did. While creating order out of chaos to make sure his army survived, Grant had been simultaneously re-setting, and the following day, they thrived – launching a counterattack that took the Confederate commanders by surprise and drove their forces from the field in confusion.

From Good to Great: The Difference

This late evening encounter, if it occurred as Sherman related, is arresting. Both men had had very similar experiences during the previous 12 hours. Both sets of experiences had been traumatic, for Grant perhaps more so, because he bore a greater responsibility for what had occurred.

Yet Sherman and Grant were in very different places. The one saw defeat, the other sensed victory. Sherman was a very fine general, but Grant was a great one. The difference is that Grant was a master of the executive's trinity: leadership, management, and command. In a business context, I call command "directing." The trinity can be thought of as three overlapping circles (Figure 6.2):

Figure 6.2: The three overlapping circles of the Executive's Trinity.

Each is a quite distinct discipline, drawing on very different qualities.

Leadership is about motivating people to achieve objectives. *Management* is about providing people with the resources they need to achieve them. *Directing* is about deciding what those objectives should be in the first place. It is an intellectual discipline, at the heart of which is *strategy* – the art of achieving a determinate goal with limited resources, against opposition, in an environment of high uncertainty.

Each aspect of the trinity demands different skills, but an organization needs all three. Most of us have a natural inclination toward one or the other, so for most of us the answer is to strive for minimal competence in them all, and put together a leadership team that can cover all the bases. Those who are outstanding at all three are rare, and therefore celebrated. Grant was one them.

Confronted with a crisis, Grant placed himself in the center of the trinity where the circles overlap, and shifted between all three so fast that he did them more or less simultaneously. War is, in fact, just a series of interlocking crises, even in a planned battle. Shiloh, which was not just unplanned but a daunting surprise, is a dramatic microcosm.

It is as if Grant's mind was a clock with three hands:

The second hand is the *leadership* hand which whirrs around: he rallies his men, supporting and encouraging his strong divisional commanders, and stepping in personally when the weak ones fail. He had the emotional discipline not to show his feelings. He hated the sight of blood so much he never ate red meat. That day he saw plenty of blood.

The minute hand is the *management* hand that ensures people get critical resources, the most urgent of which, at the beginning of the day, was ammunition. He knew they couldn't do everything at once so he sorted priorities and delegated execution.

The hour hand is the *directing* hand, which was thinking at a higher level all the time, discerning patterns and putting together a picture of the whole situation, which included the state of the enemy. This was the one that was thinking about what was out of sight – such as the bridges – and wrote the note to Buell; that, as he rallied his regiments, was also thinking about where to move them; that decided to concentrate his artillery by the river; and that positioned his reinforcements to hit back the next day. For most of his generals it was a case of what Daniel Kahneman calls WYSIATI – "what you see is all there is." Not for Grant. He overcame that and all the other usual biases.

Sherman's mind-clock just had the second hand and the minute hand. At Shiloh, that was fine, because Sherman was a divisional commander and he only needed to lead and manage. Grant was the Army commander, and he needed to direct as well. Directing only needs to be carried out by a few, but they make a huge difference.

Grant's Qualities

Born in Ohio as the son of a foreman in a tannery, Grant was a West Point graduate, trained as a soldier. His business ventures were failures. The Civil War made him, and he went on to become the 18th President of the United States. He learned to master the trinity through experience, but a few traits of character helped him.

He was modest in manner, dress, and habits. Famously unconcerned with his appearance, he ate even more simply than his staff, spoke simply and little, and hated pomp and ceremony. His ego was never going to get in the way of his dedication to his cause – the union. Not all of the great commanders were modest. But though some sought personal glory, none allowed personal interests to get in the way of achieving results. Dedication to a cause is something they all have in common.

That dedication may have strengthened another characteristic: courage. His physical courage was clear. He did not seek danger, and at Shiloh he only exposed himself to it when he had to, but when he did, he remained conspicuously unconcerned. Of possibly greater significance was his moral courage and resilience – an indifference not to danger but to setbacks. He made unpopular decisions when he felt them to be necessary.

Intellectually, Grant was comfortable with uncertainty and ambiguity, but he abhorred confusion. He constantly sought to understand reality, his mind dedicated to sense-making. Consequently, he was completely open to new information and to the ideas of others. But Grant also possessed the self-confidence to always form his own final judgments. He was a conceptual type, unconcerned with the formal processes and procedures of military life and the obsession with details that it often entails. In his dealings with subordinates he was no authoritarian. But in the end, he called the shots.

His judgments were not infallible, but most of the time he was right. For, despite his unimpressive record at school, Grant was a man of formidable intellect. He absorbed large amounts of information very quickly. He read voraciously and acquired an encyclopedic knowledge of military campaigns. He also had an eye for detail, but was very selective about which details interested him. His mind was constantly working on integrating and interpreting information, looking for patterns and boiling things down to their essence. His mind, it appeared to others, was never still. One observer noted his habit of whittling sticks with a small knife, and attributed it to a desire to occupy his hands whilst his mind was "all the while intent on other things."

Though he was highly conceptual, Grant was not a theorist. His judgments were informed by common sense. Common sense drove logic. He could reason his way through a problem with very little information while others wanted to find out more. Logic combined with pattern recognition derived from experience enabled him both to make up his mind while others hesitated, and remain comfortable with residual risk and uncertainty.

If these traits might be considered matters of disposition or character, Grant also possessed an acquired skill he honed to a very high level. It is not the first thing to come to mind in listing the core skills of the great commanders, but it is shared by all of them. Grant was a superb writer.

He wrote all his dispatches himself, often at night, often at high speed, and all were concise and clear. One staff officer once observed of Grant's orders that "no matter how hurriedly he may write them on the field, no one ever has the slightest doubt as to their meaning or even has to read them over a second time to understand them." The note Grant penned to Buell at Shiloh was one such:

> The attack on my forces has been very spirited since early this morning. The appearance of fresh troops on the field now would have a powerful effect both by inspiring our men and disheartening the enemy. If you can get upon the field, leaving all your baggage on the east bank of the river, it will be a move to our advantage and possibly save the day to us. The rebel force is estimated at over 100,000 men. My headquarters will be in the log cabin on top of the hill, where you will be furnished a staff officer, to guide you to your place on the field.

For Grant, as for most commanders, reliable information about the enemy was a rare luxury. The "estimate" of the Confederate strength is off by almost 150%. It was actually closer to 40,000. Despite that, his decisions, and the actions they implied, were clear.

What Grant Did

These characteristics, partly innate and partly acquired, are just the foundation. What is more important is how Grant chose to act. His actions on that day at Shiloh exemplify patterns of behavior which he and all the great commanders exhibit under almost all circumstances, but become critical when the situation is critical. The patterns in what they do, and what they do *not* do, set them apart from most.

As a *leader*, Grant gave good leaders support and encouragement according to their needs. Though he visited them all, he spent least time with Sherman, though his troops were raw and bore the brunt of the first attack, because Sherman needed the least help. Only when leaders failed did Grant step in and temporarily take over.

Despite that, one thing that Grant did *not* do was to issue rebukes or seek someone to blame for what occurred. He could easily have blamed his divisional subordinates for the lack of entrenchments. He chose to bear that responsibility himself. Instead of shaming failing subordinates, Grant focused everyone's efforts on getting through the day, for if they were to do so, they had to act as a team as they were, with weak members as well as strong.

That did not mean he did not notice. In the days and weeks that followed, commanders who failed were quietly sidelined. Those who stood the test of the day were given greater responsibilities, Sherman prominent among them.

In leading, the great commanders motivate people to do what is needed in the moment, build teams, and develop other leaders.

As a *manager*, Grant defined priorities throughout the day, the first being ammunition, and delegated responsibility for execution. Even as his thoughts were on strategy, Grant still paid enough attention to critical operational matters to ensure that they were being properly attended to. In his memoirs, Sherman observes that on the second day of the battle, cartridges ran out several times. "But," he adds, "General Grant had thoughtfully kept a supply coming from the rear."

Having assessed what resources were available, he organized them, but in doing so he did not attempt to do the job of the level below him. He gave the job of creating the gun battery that defeated the final attack to one of his staff officers, Colonel J.D. Webster.

Other resources, he redeployed. His cavalry were useless in the wooded terrain, so he formed them up in the rear to stop stragglers and send them back to the front as reinforcements. Some Confederate soldiers ran away too, but nobody on their side thought to do this, and so they were lost to their army. Grant found some use for everything he had. In a crisis, identifying and deploying all your resources is important.

But Grant also devoted effort to acquiring resources that were not yet available, not just to stabilize his front on that day, but to be ready for the next day. At the same time as he was taking resolute action in the "now," Grant had sufficient mental capacity to be thinking about his next move.

In managing, the great commanders make maximum use of all available resources, and gather more for tomorrow as well as today.

Which brings us to what Grant did as a *director*.

As he rode around during the day, he was integrating what he saw into an overall picture of the situation. He moved around more and so saw more than any of his subordinates did, but he also noticed things they didn't and used patterns of experience to integrate them into an overall picture of the situation. While others' minds were completely filled with their own troubles, Grant also thought about what must be going on the other side.

Everyone was struck by the ferocity and determination of the Confederate attacks. But Grant noticed that most of the attacks were uncoordinated "dashes," telling him that their units had become intermingled and their commanders were unable to direct them effectively. This lack of cohesion was a weakness he could exploit.

He knew that attacking troops become more exhausted than defending ones, that they would spend a cold, wet night in the open, and that it would be hard for them to be given food or ammunition. He saw to it that his men got both, and knew that he now had fresh troops available. It was a great opportunity to turn defeat into victory. He visited each of his subordinates during the night to make sure each one knew their part in his plan for the next day.

That opportunity existed because he had taken time out to give calm, clear direction during the day. He was very clear about his main effort. First it was holding the center, to buy time to shorten the line; then it was the defense of Pittsburg Landing; then it was deploying his reinforcements. What kind of crazy guy takes time to write a little note to one of his old college mates when his organization is disintegrating in front of his eyes? A great commander.

In directing, the great commanders form a complete picture of the overall situation, grasp its essence, and use common sense and logic to decide what to do next.

In his memoirs, Grant remarks that there was in fact "no hour during the day when I doubted the eventual defeat of the enemy." As he steadily worked on building up an advantage, there was one thing he did not do. Give up.

After Shiloh, the northern press vilified Grant for being caught by surprise. There were stories that he was drunk and that Buell had saved the day. When Pennsylvania politician Alexander McClure visited the President late one night to demand that Grant be dismissed, Lincoln sat silent in his chair for a while before gathering himself up to reply: "I can't spare this man. He fights."

Others did not fight. Some fought and lost. Grant fought and won. He won because he was not just a great manager who understood logistics, nor a great leader who could inspire his staff and his men, nor just a great director who grasped the essentials of strategy – but a master of the trinity.

Roselinde Torres, Martin Reeves, Peter Tollman,
Christian Veith

Chapter 7
The Rewards of CEO Reflection

CEOs live on a nonstop treadmill. They are under constant pressure to perform, live in a 24-7 spotlight of social-media attention, and swim in a deep pool of information. One CEO told us that she had received some 1,000 pieces of advice during her early days as the chief executive.

Corporate organizations are more complex than ever before. BCG's "index of complicatedness" of major companies has been rising by nearly 7% per year for the past 50 years. Deep thought and reflection are casualties of this high-pressure and high-stakes environment as CEOs rush from event to event and decision to decision. Downtime is often regarded as wasted time.

CEOs who do make time to reflect, however, say that it is time well spent, and our research on CEO success validates that view. Reflection leads to better insights into innovation, strategy, and execution. Reflection gives rise to better outcomes and higher credibility with corporate boards, leadership teams, workforces, and other stakeholders.

The most famous and successful practitioner of reflection is, perhaps, Warren Buffett, who says that he spends about six hours a day reading. "He has a lot of time to think," says his partner Charlie Munger. "You look at his schedule sometimes, and there's a haircut. Tuesday: Haircut day." Tuesday, in other words, is a thinking day.

Most CEOs do not have the luxury of limiting their daily calendar to a single act of reflection, but many of them could spend more time reflecting. It takes discipline, practice, and structure, but by routinely setting aside time in their calendars, CEOs can reap the rewards of reflection.

The Value of Reflection

Reflective thinking is thinking turned in on itself. In reflective thought, a person examines underlying assumptions, core beliefs, and knowledge. Unlike critical thought, which is aimed at solving a problem and achieving a specific outcome, reflective thought enhances the framing of problems, the search for meaning, and pattern recognition. Mary Helen Immordino-Yang, an associate professor of education, psychology, and neuroscience at the University of Southern California,

https://doi.org/10.1515/9783110775174-007

has written about the role of "constructive internal reflection" in "making meaning of new information and for distilling creative, emotionally relevant connections between complex ideas."

Reflective thinking engages the medial prefrontal cortex, the part of the brain involved in self-referential mental activities. At rest, this region exhibits the highest metabolic activity and during goal-oriented thinking, lower levels of activity. In other words, reflective thinking and critical thinking exist at opposite ends of a digital switch. When one is "on," the other is "off."

CEOs should engage in both types of thinking. As complexity rises and the pace of change accelerates, CEOs need to engage in critical thinking to solve immediate challenges and in reflective thinking to clarify the big picture and imagine untapped opportunities.

The Roadblocks to Reflection

The world of business is typically seen as the world of action. Leaders *drive* performance and *deliver* results. Action indisputably makes the world go around. But it is important not to mistake motion for effectiveness. Computer scientist Cal Newport writes that many people mistakenly view "busyness as a proxy for productivity."

Signs of busyness abound. A 2011 Harvard Business School study showed that CEOs spend 60% of their time in meetings and 25% on the phone or at public events, leaving 15% for everything else, including travel, email, reading, and reflection.

This busyness has a cognitive cost. The human brain has natural limits in its ability to pay attention, remember, and process information. Multitasking breaches those limits faster.

One of the large challenges for CEOs is breaking away from the busyness – the necessary formalities of being CEO – in order to reflect. CEOs cannot lead monastic lives, but they can learn to be organized and disciplined about engaging in deep thought. For those who practice it, reflection can become routine.

The Three Rules of Reflection

How do busy people find the time to reflect and derive the most benefit from the investment? Our advisory work with CEOs has shown that three factors facilitate insightful reflection.

1. A Structure and a Schedule

Unstructured and unguided thought tends to dwell on immediate worries and familiar conundrums rather than fundamental and foundational issues. Thought focused on solving immediate problems is critical – not reflective – thought. Reflective thought sets the stage for long-term success.

Time for reflection should be a regularly scheduled and protected event on the CEO's calendar. With discipline, CEOs can learn how to reflect on their own. In our work with CEOs, we have discovered that they can acquire the foundational habits and practices of reflective thought in as little as 14 hours.

Reflection is a skill that keeps on giving. Once CEOs learn the skill, they can practice on their own or with somebody they trust. One CEO told us, "It has been very valuable for me not to be beholden to anyone and still gain a structured approach on issues."

To help CEOs establish the foundation for reflection, we lead them through a series of questions on strategy, organization, leadership, and personal vision. The following is a sampling of core questions from our work with one CEO:

- Are there underlying patterns within your company or industry that are rarely acknowledged?
- What are your intuitions and hunches about potential sources for new value creation?
- What new business models from outside your industry intrigue you?
- If you could start with a blank slate, how would you describe the ideal culture of your organization? How does that ideal compare with your actual culture?
- What is the conception of success and the leadership style that you would like to convey?
- What are the unstated and less refined ambitions and dreams – both personal and professional – that you would like to achieve?

2. A Trusted Dialogue Partner

A CEO has to maintain a persona. In front of their people, CEOs need to project confidence, optimism, and command. In public – and even with their most senior executives – they rarely exhibit signs of self-doubt, admit uncertainty, or question core beliefs. Scrutiny in social media amplifies this tendency toward heroic stoicism.

Reflection, on the other hand, requires introspection and honesty that are difficult for CEOs to convey in their day-to-day activities. Having spent their careers hitting targets and achieving other outward signs of success, CEOs themselves may be uncomfortable with the idea of reflection.

To inspire and refine objective, reflective thought, a CEO can benefit from conversations with a trusted partner who is deeply steeped in the industry and with whom the CEO is comfortable being frank and open. If their relationship is strong, this partner can prompt the CEO with questions, observations, and challenges.

An effective dialogue partner needs both counseling skills and knowledge of the CEO's industry *and* organizational context: the partner's advice must be grounded in the CEO's specific situation. The partner and the CEO can flip back and forth between the big picture and the details, surfacing links among strategy, organization, and leadership topics. In other words, an effective dialogue partner can mirror the CEO's thinking.

This combination of content and counseling ensures that the reflection ultimately informs value creation. One CEO told his dialogue partner, "You combine empathy and uncompromising guidance. Your experience in the industry really came out in our discussions."

3. A Catalytic Conversation

Many executives and other stakeholders who meet with the CEO want to focus on their own agenda or are simply executing the CEO's agenda. Their conversations are a critical part of corporate life, but they are unlikely to lead to reflective thought.

Dialogue partners bring an entirely different mindset and set of materials to their discussions with CEOs. CEOs benefit from new and unbiased information in order to stimulate and catalyze their thinking. By having an independent eye-level relationship with a CEO, a dialogue partner can provide perspectives that otherwise are unlikely to be aired. These may include case studies that demonstrate disruption or pivotal leadership decisions; scenarios that ground thinking in the past, present, and future; and frameworks that challenge conventional thinking and ways of working. One CEO told us that in our work with him, he had found our "insights to be truly valuable to my thinking, and they propelled my ability to deliver on the right outcomes."

The Clarity of Reflection

Reflection is anything but passive. It leads to insight, action, engagement, and emotional commitment. CEOs confirm that the time spent reflecting on their business and organization produces positive results. In our work with CEOs, the insights that they have generated during reflective thought form the basis of a 12-month plan with quarterly commitments that are built into their calendars.

CEOs say that structured reflection helps them make bold moves, avoid crises such as proxy fights, and establish the sequence and pace for delivering the most value. "I feel good about this course of action because I've really thought it through," one CEO told us.

On a personal level, CEOs have told us that structured reflection has helped them manage the demands of the job more effectively because they have learned to allocate time and energy more intelligently. "In the past," one CEO said, "I was more operationally focused. This CEO role gives me the opportunity to be more strategic and visionary. I need to think differently to change."

During a CEO's typical day, finding time to reflect can be challenging. It's not possible to reflect in 15-minute increments, and it's not productive to reflect and then forget the insights that were generated. According to one CEO, structured reflection "has been driving what we have been doing in the corporation as a whole."

The reflective CEO is a productive CEO who is capable of both imagining and executing rewarding strategies.

Andrew Dyer, Elena Barybkina, C. Patrick Erker, Jeff Sullivan
Chapter 8
A CEO's Guide to Leading and Learning in the Digital Age

Imagine: You have gathered your employees in a conference room for a routine meeting. Suddenly, the doors are thrown open and one of those idiomatic 800-pound gorillas enters – and claims – the space. This particular 800-pound gorilla has a name: *Digital*. And digital is not going to get back into its cage.

The arrival of digital is a major upheaval – a chest-beating threat to traditional ways of working. As more and more jobs are automated, employees and governments worry about unemployment – or worse, unemployability. And as digital introduces new opportunities, employers worry about finding employees to pursue them. Nearly half of US and German companies reported the lack of qualified employees[1] as the biggest constraint to a full digital transformation. You're the CEO and it's up to you to respond to all these concerns. *What are you going to do?*

This disruption requires that people and enterprises adopt new ways of working. And that requires an innovative approach to learning at work. Learning is survival-critical for employees and enterprises alike. If you fail to establish new ways of learning, you can't achieve new ways of working; and absent those, you can't compete. To avoid that fate in the digital age, you need an adaptable learning ecosystem that elevates learning strategy to the CEO level and embraces digital.

The New "Workscape"

The world is poised for what is likely to be the most disruptive change since the Industrial Revolution. On the one hand, digital is creating a need for employees with a fresh set of skills, and employers are struggling to find and retain that talent. And on the other, artificial intelligence, virtual reality, and machine learning will continue to produce machines capable not only of completing simple tasks but of commandeering the creative and intellectual work that

---

1 https://www.bcg.com/publications/2017/people-organization-strategy-twelve-forces-radically-change-organizations-work.

https://doi.org/10.1515/9783110775174-008

humans have long considered theirs alone. There are many predictions about the number of jobs automated or unfilled and the percentage of employees whose jobs are threatened. One such prediction foresees a potential impact of $10 trillion[2] in lost GDP over 20 years from skill imbalances. Regardless of the exact numbers, CEOs need to recognize that the coming change is real, enormous, and game changing.

Projections about job losses can make for a gloomy employment outlook. One view is that the rise of digital is inexorably reducing the need for some employees and the roles of others. Another view: the rise of digital won't necessarily lead to the elimination of employees; rather, it will force a reexamination and reimagining of the best ways for humans to deliver value to organizations. They will still be employees, but they'll be doing different jobs[3] – like scrum master or digital venture strategist – in different ways. This will mean identifying particular knowledge, skills, and mindsets that require the "human touch."

We subscribe to that second, more optimistic view: it's appropriate – and crucial – to redefine employee roles amid, throughout, and beyond the impending digital change. It will probably be messy, like all change. But as with all good change efforts, it's critical that CEOs get ahead of the change and shape it, rather than let their organizations be shaped by it.

Technology is not just transforming and overtaking work tasks. It is also part of a confluence of forces, including socioeconomic trends and the adoption of agile, that are changing ways of working. Freelance employment and the gig economy are on the rise. Employees are increasingly pushed toward self-directed models that emphasize autonomy, and mobile work is becoming more common. In many cases, employees can do their jobs anytime, anywhere. A redefinition of work, and learning at work, must be considered against this backdrop.

The New "Learnscape": Learning in the Workflow

Alongside the changes in ways of working, the world is experiencing shifts in ways of learning. Learning and education once consisted of classroom instruction, rote memorization, and capstones such as high school graduation. But in a world of dynamic change, learning must become more dynamic too.

---

2 https://www.bcg.com/publications/2014/people-organization-human-resources-global-workforce-crisis.
3 https://www.bcg.com/publications/2017/people-organization-technology-how-gain-develop-digital-talent-skills.

Current education systems and training models cannot provide employees with reliable, lasting skills. By the time students graduate from college and join the workforce, many of the skills they have learned are already out of date, given the blistering pace of change. This means that learning can no longer happen in the first decades of life in preparation for the rest of life; rather, the best employees will be learning throughout their lives, and this learning will take place at work.

To meet these evolving educational needs, CEOs should initiate what we call "learning in the workflow," and these efforts must be:
- Adaptive and personalized to individual users and their specific needs
- Always-on, with real-time support and feedback
- "Gamified," with social elements that create "learner pull" to encourage learners to participate
- Measurable, translating to outcomes both for the learners and for the enterprise

The fact that ways of working are changing provides a prime opening to introduce innovative ways of learning as well. Employees are becoming accustomed to change, to self-direction, and to a different relationship with employers and managers (who will each serve new roles in advancing learning). It's now more possible than ever to create learning-on-the-job paradigms that mesh education and employment and emphasize lifelong learning, preparing individuals for the ongoing changes.

How to Access Digital-Age Skills

Enterprises that are in need of a digital-age skill set can access it in four main ways. They can buy it (by hiring employees with the needed skills), borrow it (by engaging temporary or contract employees), open-source it (by tapping the gig economy), or build it (by developing the skills in-house).

Buying, borrowing, and open-sourcing probably seem like the quickest and simplest solutions, but the required skills are already in heavy demand. So these solutions will be increasingly elusive and, as a result, prohibitively expensive.

We believe that *building* the required skills is a critical component of an enterprise's strategy and that it will deliver the biggest payoff. It lets an organization hone precisely the skills it needs in ways that will work effectively for its organization without the growing pains of integrating new employees, and it sets the stage for the extension of those skills. Building the skills in-house also sidesteps the cost of simply hiring new people for new roles. (Research has shown that highly paid jobs can have turnover costs of 200% of salary.[4])

As the marketplace continues to evolve and call for up-to-date skills, employees need to find a place to acquire the necessary learning opportunities. Enterprises that address this need can make a learning ecosystem part of their value proposition to attract and retain employees. And when an employer demonstrates dedication to its workforce by investing in education and development, it gains some measure of employee loyalty.

Once a CEO and leadership team decide to build a learning ecosystem, the effort must be comprehensive and deliberate: it must address learning for all employees, be planned in a way that integrates corporate strategy, and have clear metrics as well as rewards for both the enterprise and the employees. It must be adaptable to scenarios where humans work with robots side by side or in some kind of hierarchical relationship. And it must be designed for inevitable change. An adaptable and flexible learning ecosystem will allow for perpetual learning as it too learns and adapts.

A New Learning Ecosystem and the Pillars that Support it

No one can offer a one-size-fits-all solution for enterprises that need to build a learning ecosystem; certainly, customization will be needed at every level. In fact, we don't believe that a one-size-fits-all solution exists; given the ongoing rapid change, such a solution might always be a moving target, and appropriately so.

With that in mind, one tenet of any enterprise's approach to learning must be an emphasis on the know-how rather than the simplistic know-what. The learning ecosystem must maintain a focus on this overarching goal: learner-employees need to learn not only specific skills but also the ability to think critically about how to adapt and extrapolate those skills.

Of course, the development of learning ecosystems has already begun, so we can offer some insight into the pathways to success. The new learning ecosystem approach that we envision has particular characteristics, approaches, and tools. It will have a presence at all levels of the organization, with the

---

4 Center for American Progress (2012), *There Are Significant Business Costs to Replacing Employees,* https://www.americanprogress.org/wp-content/uploads/2012/11/CostofTurnover.pdf.

consistent involvement of the CEO. It will incorporate digital considerations and digital approaches to learning. We envision this deliberate construction as a house (see Figure 8.1). The overarching strategy, which tightly combines business strategy with learning strategy, gives rise to specific learning offerings. The enablers are a foundation for the offerings, and are championed by the CEO.

Source: BCG.

Figure 8.1: A comprehensive, enterprise-wide learning ecosystem.

Building an effective learning ecosystem requires adherence to a set of essential principles that are relevant throughout and fundamental to creating success:

– **Learning is a CEO issue.** A large-scale, digitally oriented reskilling initiative is a core aspect of continual transformation and requires the CEO's attention. That attention doesn't stop once high-level strategy has been established. The CEO must be involved throughout.
– **Learning must become part of daily rhythms and routines.** Employers designing learning ecosystems should resist the temptation to rely too heavily on traditional learning models, like online courses, and instead develop experiential programs that encourage learners to get used to learning while on the job.
– **Learning has to be embedded in the workflow.** There are four essential elements (noted earlier) that must always be present for this to work: the learning must be adaptable, the employees must have constant access to their learning on the job, lessons should incorporate games and be social, and the learning must be measurable.

- **Employers and employees should enter into a 21st-century "learning contract."** An agreement – a new kind of social contract for learning – must be in place to outline the ways in which employees and the enterprise will share accountability for learning and align on the pathways and skills in that learning.
- **Managers must transform from taskmasters to learning coaches.** Managers, in a new role, will have the responsibility and capacity to communicate to employees the skills that have value because they contribute to achieving corporate goals.
- **Learning strategies must leverage insights from the cognitive and behavioral sciences.** Cutting-edge neuroscience is revealing insights about the way people learn, leading to new techniques that are designed to build on human motivations and learning processes. Learning programs[5] are already taking advantage of these brain science techniques with efficient and influential innovations such as badges to mark progress through multi-part tasks and "digital nudges"[6] to encourage behavioral change. This is an active space: education companies are using techniques such as the spacing effect, retrieval practice, and confidence-based learning to improve outcomes.
- **Learning must focus on traditionally relevant as well as new skills.** The impetus for building the learning ecosystem is the need to teach employees about the latest digital technologies and help them develop new digital skills. But some traditional skills are evergreen (like problem solving, communications, and data analysis) and remain relevant; the learning ecosystem should advance these skills, too.
- **Enterprises must offer recognition to learner-employees.** This principle applies throughout the ecosystem because it encompasses so much: recognizing and respecting the needs and inputs of each employee, providing incentives for learning, and positioning the employer as an issuer of credentials, providing certifications that signal individuals' valuable accomplishments and prowess to those inside and outside the enterprise.

It's both possible and imperative to create a successful learning ecosystem. That kind of learning is something we experience in our own company. Our Learning at BCG (LAB) program is a fundamental component of our recruiting, retention, and development strategies throughout the organization and around

---

5 https://www.bcg.com/capabilities/people-strategy/learning-programs.
6 https://www.bcg.com/publications/2017/people-organization-operations-persuasive-power-digital-nudge.

the world. We all participate in training on a variety of topics year-round, and this program helps us with professional and personal development.

Of course, no workplace learning program can or should be an entirely altruistic offering designed simply to ensure that employees have up-to-date skills that keep them marketable. It's also true that leaders have an obligation to leave their enterprises stronger and more capable than they were when they inherited them. This mandate includes a responsibility to employees and a broader societal obligation to advance development and well-being. Thus, though building a comprehensive digital-age learning ecosystem is a daunting task, doing so is essential for reasons both mission-critical and altruistic.

But remember that digital is an indispensable aid to the development of your perpetual-learning system. The ecosystem you create will incorporate learning about digital and about working alongside intelligent machines, and it will use digital learning approaches. When it comes to leading and learning in the digital age, a savvy CEO can and should make the 800-pound gorilla an ally by harnessing its power to improve learning and prepare for change.

Peter Tollman, Joshua Serlin, Michelle Akers, Anson Dorrance

Chapter 9
The Power of Inspiration, Perspiration, and Cooperation – In Sports and in Business

We play for each other.

This guiding philosophy of the 1990s US women's national soccer team – as articulated by Anson Dorrance, its coach during the first half of the decade – propelled the squad to unparalleled success. The team won the inaugural Women's World Cup in 1991 and the first gold medal awarded to a women's soccer squad at the 1996 Olympics. It concluded the decade by defeating China in the thrilling 1999 World Cup final.

The team did not just win the big games but dominated throughout the decade, compiling a remarkable record of 155 wins, 21 losses, and 9 ties while outscoring opponents by an average of three goals per game. "We wanted to dominate, to crush every single team every single minute of every single game, as individuals and as a team," said Michelle Akers, one of the star players.

The team was notable not just for its victories. The players redefined the role of women in sports, fighting for gender equality, equal pay, and the reputation of women's soccer. They willingly subjected themselves to brutal training and conditioning sessions in order to attain those goals.

"They can be credited with nothing less than the founding of women's soccer as an international game," wrote Sally Jenkins in *The Washington Post*. "The worst that could be said of them was that they were joyous carousers. They were one of the few things left in sports you could watch without suspicion."

How many businesses and organizations today have been equally dominant? How many can say that their employees truly "play for each other" and for a higher purpose? In our experience, not many. To be sure, the US squad had stars, such as Akers and Mia Hamm, but the stars themselves attributed their success to team alchemy.

Playing for each other is what happens at effective organizations. In these institutions, people cooperate – they seek group success over individual attainment and accomplish more than the sum of their individual achievements. Unfortunately, this happens infrequently because few organizations are designed to promote cooperation.

A BCG approach called *smart simplicity* unlocks organizational effectiveness by systematically encouraging cooperation. While hard to achieve,

https://doi.org/10.1515/9783110775174-009

cooperation is easy to see in the success of such dominating sports teams as the Golden State Warriors, the New England Patriots, Bayern Munich, and the All Blacks, New Zealand's national men's rugby team.

We chose sports teams as the canvas to show how other organizations can promote cooperation and improve performance because of sports' consistent rules and binary outcomes. We chose the US women's soccer team of the 1990s, specifically, because it was arguably more successful for a longer period than any team in any other sport.

The Mess Facing Organizations Today

Most businesses and organizations do not perform close to their peak potential, and even when they do, they struggle to sustain that level of performance, especially in today's climate. We know this empirically through shorter corporate lifespans and rising volatility rates (see Figure 9.1).

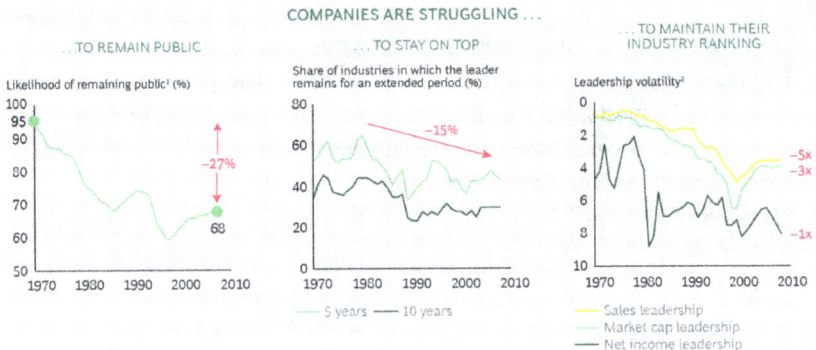

1One-year likelihood of delisting calculated as percentage of 35,000 publicly listed companies that ceased stock market trading in each calendar year. Delisting is an outcome of bankruptcy, merger, acquisition, going private, or other factors.
2Average change in industry ranking per year of companies in 69 industries.
Sources: CaplQ; BCG Henderson Institute analysis: BCG ValueScience Center analysis.

Figure 9.1: Strong performance is increasingly hard to sustain.

We also know it in our gut. High-performing organizations are buzzing with activity, excitement, and possibility. Teams work together – they cooperate – to achieve common objectives. But at many organizations, the lethargy is palpable. People are motivated, just not on the job. They apply their talents in their hobbies and volunteer work, or with their friends and family.

Why do great things happen so seldom or so fleetingly at so many large organizations? One major reason is that most organizations still rely on outmoded management theories born of the assembly line. These theories were developed in a simpler time when most work was rote and precision was more important to organizational success than critical thinking. They assume that people are the weak link and need to be controlled through rules (the "hard" approach) or through team-building activities such as offsite retreats, affiliation events, and even lunchtime yoga classes designed to foster camaraderie (the "soft" approach).

These approaches to management may have been effective when most work was algorithmic – routine – based on following a set of rules. But thanks to increasing competition, globalization, digitization, and regulation, today's economy is far more complex. Business problems have become more dynamic, and ambiguity and uncertainty have grown. Work has become heuristic, an exercise in problem solving requiring intelligent judgments and the resolution of often contradictory requirements.

Heuristic work is responsible for 70% of new-job growth in the US today. For this type of work, people cannot simply fall back on rules, because the nature of the work requires the interpretation of rules – and there are no rules to interpret the rules. In fact, rules have become counterproductive, creating bureaucracy, hindering cooperation, and frustrating employees.

A Smarter and Simpler Approach

Smart simplicity is an antidote to organizational complexity, bureaucracy, and lethargy. It unlocks latent energy and enthusiasm by encouraging cooperation.

Thomas Edison once said that genius is 1% inspiration and 99% perspiration. That famous quote misses the critical role that cooperation played at his labs, which were populated by teams of "muckers" – tinkerers, machinists, and scientists who collectively tested, tweaked, and built his inventions. When cooperation, inspiration, and perspiration come together – as they did in Edison's labs, and with the US women's soccer team in the 1990s – great things happen.

The role of leaders today is to provide inspiration while encouraging perspiration and, ultimately, cooperation. Inspiration gives people a reason to perspire – to work their butts off. But inspiration and perspiration are not enough to break through the entrenched bureaucracies of most large organizations. People, teams, and entire organizational units also need to work together, since few of today's complex problems can be solved by individuals acting independently. Hence the need for cooperation.

People are not irrationally uncooperative. They behave the way they do in order to meet individual objectives and are influenced by the resources and limitations of their workplace – or what we call *context*. There are always good reasons for their behavior – even when, if viewed from the perspective of the organization and its goals, that behavior appears irrational or dysfunctional.

Smart simplicity encourages cooperation, not by attempting to control people or force them to behave differently, but by understanding their objectives and changing the work context in such a way that cooperation becomes a rational goal. By shaping context, leaders can inspire, foster hard work, encourage cooperation – and achieve incredible results (see Box 9.1: Six Simple Rules).

Box 9.1: Six Simple Rules

Shaping context may seem abstract, but it was exactly what happened during the magical run of the US women's soccer team in the 1990s.

1. **Understand what your people really do**
   Analyze the work context to understand what people actually do and why they do it. With this understanding, you can use the other rules to foster cooperation.

2. **Reinforce integrators**
   Identify roles whose success depends on fostering cooperation across the organization, and then support those roles with the resources they need to be successful.

3. **Increase the total quantity of power**
   Figure out ways to give people more power without taking power away from others.

4. **Increase reciprocity**
   Make each person's success dependent on the success of others.

5. **Extend the shadow of the future**
   Create direct feedback loops that expose people to the consequences of their actions.

6. **Reward those who cooperate**
   Provide greater opportunities, recognition, or financial rewards to those who cooperate, and punish those who fail to do so.

Lessons from the Team

The US women's victory over Norway to win the 1991 World Cup was a wakeup call for more storied soccer nations that had long dominated the men's game. Traditional powerhouses such as Brazil and Germany dedicated themselves to building world-class women's teams. But despite their efforts, the US women kept winning, culminating in the victory over China in the 1999 World Cup.

Two head coaches and a rotating cast of supporting players were responsible for this dynasty.

Two of the contributors to this article were integral members of that team, and we rounded out their perspectives and experiences with multiple in-depth interviews with other team leaders, including captains Julie Foudy and Carla Overbeck; Lauren Gregg, an assistant coach during the 1990s; and Tiffany Roberts, a key reserve. We also interviewed members of winning men's teams, such as Bayern Munich (see Box 9.2: The People We Interviewed).

Box 9.2: The People We Interviewed

Julie Foudy was a member of the US women's national soccer team from 1987 to 2004, its co-captain from 1991 to 2000, and its captain from 2000 to 2004. She chose a career in soccer rather than medicine after her graduation from Stanford University and now works as an ESPN broadcaster.

Lauren Gregg played on the 1986 national team and was assistant coach on the squad from 1989 to 2000, serving briefly as head coach in 1997 and 2000. She was also the head coach of the women's soccer team at the University of Virginia for ten years.

Philipp Lahm was captain of Bayern Munich, the professional team he played for during most of his career. He also captained the German national team when it won the 2014 FIFA World Cup and is considered one of the greatest defensive players of all time.

Carla Overbeck was a three-time All-American selection at the University of North Carolina, a member of the national team from 1988 to 2000, and a co-captain (with Foudy) in the 1990s. She is currently an assistant women's soccer coach at Duke University.

Tiffany Roberts was selected for the national team in 1994, when she was 16 years old, and played through 2003. She is currently the head coach of the University of Central Florida women's soccer team.

Provide a Higher Calling

The interviews revealed three distinct practices, all grounded in the six simple rules, that fostered cooperation among the team's members. They worked well on the field, and they can likewise take hold in executive suites, on shop floors, and in field organizations.

Organizations extol the virtues of a clear mission and vision. While clarity is important, the ambition itself must be resonant and uplifting. For most employees, revenue targets and profit margins are not reasons to get up in the morning. Leaders must give them an authentic higher calling, a mission that inspires – not corporate gobbledygook.

Anson Dorrance became the national team coach in 1986, one year after the team's founding as a somewhat ragtag collection of largely unknown players.

In the early years, they subsisted on $10-a-day meal money, traveled to distant games by bus, stayed in cheap hotels, and wore uniforms with ironed-on names and numbers.

Despite this humble origin story, Dorrance was able to instill a higher purpose by establishing goals that transcended wins and losses. As an American raised overseas, he wanted to show the world that the US could not be kicked around on the soccer field.

Akers remembers Dorrance telling the team, "Every time you step on the field you're selling the game, changing minds, and changing the culture of what is possible for women and for everyone."

Dorrance selected a group of teenagers that included Foudy, Hamm, Overbeck, Brandi Chastain, Joy Fawcett, and Kristine Lilly – "joyous carousers" who embraced this higher calling. "It wasn't really for us. It was for the future of women's soccer," Overbeck recalled.

The team fought with the US Soccer Federation to receive pay equal to that of the men's team. Nine players, including Foudy, Overbeck, and Akers, were briefly locked out of training camp before the 1996 Olympics over the dispute. But the struggle helped galvanize the team. "We decided that, if we were going to get something done, we all had to be together," Overbeck said.

On the field, Dorrance and his team did not just want to win; they wanted to crush their opponents, who viewed the US as a second-class soccer nation. "I was going to beat them with the tools of the American spirit," Dorrance said. This translated into a simple but incredibly demanding strategy: the US would double every player on the opposing team, requiring players to train tirelessly in practice and on their own. As Akers put it, "We had a culture of 'extra' – doing whatever it took to be the best. I trained harder knowing that my teammates were doing the same thing and that this was what it would take to accomplish our goals."

Dorrance demanded that his players be in shape from day one. Early on, a player failed a training drill on the first day. Dorrance sent her home that evening. After that, no player arrived at practice out of shape for the remainder of his tenure.

These aspirations increased reciprocity (the fourth of the six simple rules), and therefore cooperation, in two important ways. First, they were audacious and beyond the reach of any single player. They made it rational for each player to subsume her individual goals to the team's shared objectives. Second, they motivated each player to devote every ounce of effort to the team's interests. That's what led Akers, for example, to endure over 30 orthopedic surgeries during her career. "Each of us had a role to play to help the team win. Part of mine was being the target for opposing teams." Rather than shy away from this role, Akers embraced it. "By serving as the target, I could help others play more freely," she said. "The more challenging it was, the more fun it was, and the better I got, so bring it on."

These aspirations also extended the shadow of the future (the fifth rule). Players who failed to cooperate or who gave less than 100% damaged the team's chances of winning and put at risk the larger goals of gender equality and women's participation in sports.

Make it Clear that Every Player – Even the 20th – Matters

For reciprocity and cooperation to occur and for the higher calling to have meaning, players have to believe that their roles matter. This is not easy on a soccer team, where strict substitution rules limit the playing time of reserves. How do coaches keep players engaged when their role may not seem important?

This is not easy in business, either. It can be hard to motivate middle managers and frontline employees, who often don't see how their efforts contribute to the larger purpose of the organization. But without the engagement of these players and employees, teams and organizations will fall short of their goals.

It's not just a matter of paying lip service. Negativity can spread quickly on a sports team, especially among players who spend most of their time on the bench. The coaches of the US team were keenly aware of this challenge, which they aptly referred to as "engaging the 20th player." The engagement – and ultimate success – of the entire team depended on the engagement of each member. One way the US coaches achieved buy-in from reserves was to elevate the importance of practice relative to games. As Gregg and Dorrance put it, games were simply an outcome of the training that occurred in practice.

Tiffany Roberts, all five-foot-five-inches and 120 pounds of her, joined the team as an inexperienced 16-year-old but quickly made her mark through tenacious play in practice. Roberts' gritty play "helped other players improve," Gregg recalled. "She elevated the practice."

Roberts' selection didn't just pay off in practice. In the semifinals of the 1996 Olympics against Norway, Tony DiCicco (Dorrance's successor, who died in 2017) started Roberts and asked her to play a new position and to hound Hege Riise, the best player in Norway at the time, and arguably in the world. By neutralizing Riise, DiCicco hoped to win a 10-on-10 game. It worked. Roberts shut down Riise, and the US went on to win the semifinal match and eventually the Olympic gold medal. "It felt really good to know how much my team trusted me in such a big job," Roberts said.

Even reserves who had lost their starting jobs bought in to the mission of the team. Dorrance remembers overhearing midfielder Tracey Bates talking to her mother on the phone about losing her starting job to Lilly, five years her junior. "Don't you understand, Kristine is better than I am," Dorrance recalled Bates telling her mother.

Even when they did not play in a game, reserves received praise for their roles on the sideline. Akers described how coaches complimented bench players who ran water bottles to the starters during breaks. This mentality led to a running joke that the players were "socialists." Joking aside, the focus on the 20th player increased reciprocity and cooperation. In other words, "whether I am the 20th player or a key player, whether I am a substitute or I start, whether I assist or I score, my role matters," Gregg said.

Walk in One Another's Shoes

Cooperation requires that leaders and coworkers understand what the other really does (the first rule). Otherwise, it's impossible for people to understand how to work together most effectively and for leaders to know which behaviors to encourage and reward.

The coaches of the US team encouraged this understanding in several ways. First, Dorrance meticulously tracked individual performance on the field. He refers to this tracking of individual performance as a "competitive cauldron," which he then sought to balance with off-the-field camaraderie. "What's critical for me as a coach is to recruit every single element to drive performance," he said. He also wanted to understand the "internal narrative" of his players, the beliefs about themselves that both motivated and inhibited them. So he asked players to rank themselves on a 1 to 5 scale on such attributes as self-discipline, competitive fire, self-belief, love of playing the game, love of watching the game, and grit. "The first step in player development is for the player to figure out who she is," Dorrance said. "A great way to unlock potential is to get the player as close to the truth of her internal narrative as possible."

Second, in pregame meetings, coaches carefully tied the individual responsibilities of each player, including the reserves, to the broader objectives of the team. Players understood why their role – no matter how seemingly insignificant – mattered.

Finally, the coaches created "small societies," player groupings – the "attacking front six" or the "defensive back four," for instance – that had to work together effectively to help the team win. Dorrance borrowed this concept from the great Argentinian coach César Luis Menotti. The coaches set specific objectives that could only be achieved if each small society worked together as a unit.

In the men's game, Pep Guardiola, one of the most successful coaches of all time, used a similar technique to encourage cooperation. He would force players to play out of position in both practices and games. Philipp Lahm, who served as captain under Guardiola at Bayern Munich, says the tactic taught his teammates "the role of the other," the ability to see the game from different perspectives and the value of sacrifice for the greater good.

These practices all engendered a shared sense of responsibility and a desire to work together – and may have rescued the 1999 season from defeat. In the early minutes of the 1999 World Cup quarterfinals match against Germany, a routine pass by Brandi Chastain back to goalie Brianna Scurry squirted into the US goal. On a team of me-first players, such a mistake could have broken everyone's spirit, but Gregg and Akers remember that it galvanized the squad. Overbeck came to Chastain's side, not to berate but to encourage. "I wanted to make sure I got to Brandi first and told her it was going to be okay," Overbeck said. "It's over. There is nothing you can do about it. We need you, now more than ever."

Chastain went on to tie the game at the end of the first half. Two rounds later, Chastain scored one of the most iconic goals in women's soccer history – the final penalty kick against China – to win the World Cup for the US in what remains the most watched women's sporting event in history.

To be sure, the US team experienced failure, falling in the semifinals to Norway in the 1995 World Cup, for example. But it was a failure of cooperation, not a failure of talent. Recalling the 1996 team that won gold, Foudy said, "When we got on the field we were very intense, but off the field we were always pulling pranks and messing around. The year before, we had talent on the team, but we didn't have the joy or the unity."

Let's be clear. Sports and business are different activities, and metaphors that attempt to connect the two are often artificial. There is a joy and camaraderie in sports that is hard to find in business. One involves play; the other, work.

But cooperation is essential – and the same – in both activities. Cooperation is less about huddling together and rallying behind the coach than it is about leaders providing a context in which teamwork and individual self-sacrifice can occur.

At a time when the structural advantages of companies and entire industries are diminishing owing to digital disruption and other forces, leaders can still rely on what they profess to be their most valuable asset: their people. Not by directing or controlling them but by unleashing their latent talents. That ultimately is the lesson of the US women's soccer team of the 1990s.

Part III: **New Leadership Challenges**

Martin Reeves, Johann D. Harnoss

Chapter 10
The Business of Business Is No Longer Just Business

Yesterday, love was such an easy game to play.
— Paul McCartney, 1965

Many business leaders have spent their careers in times of relative economic predictability and political stability, punctuated by occasional market downturns. As a consequence, they have been able to focus on activities that are directly related to the "business of business," such as competitive strategy, innovation, operations, and human resources.

In hindsight, yesterday's business game was a relatively easy one to play.

Leaders today increasingly find themselves in unfamiliar territory marked by high levels of uncertainty and instability, a global economy that is growing more slowly, and new political realities. These change the relationship between business and other parts of society; they also have profound implications for strategy and competitive advantage.

Political and Economic Uncertainty Matters

Today's multidimensional uncertainty is in part a byproduct of two important drivers of economic growth in the past 40 years: global economic integration and technological innovation. Together, they have increased global prosperity but have also contributed to inequality within countries, giving rise to protectionist policies that directly affect trade, taxation, and talent mobility.[1] The two forces have also coupled societies, economies, and businesses more intricately than ever before.

In this tightly intertwined world, companies feel the impact of political and economic factors more acutely. A recent BCG Henderson Institute analysis applying natural language processing (NLP) to S&P 500 companies' investor communications shows that many executives now devote more attention to reacting to and shaping political and economic issues (see Figure 10.1).

---

1 Reeves, M., and J. Harnoss, "An Agenda for the Future of Global Business," hbr.org, February 27, 2017, https://www.bcg.com/publications/2017/strategy-agenda-for-future-global-business.

https://doi.org/10.1515/9783110775174-010

BCG Politics and Economics Index, 2005 = 100

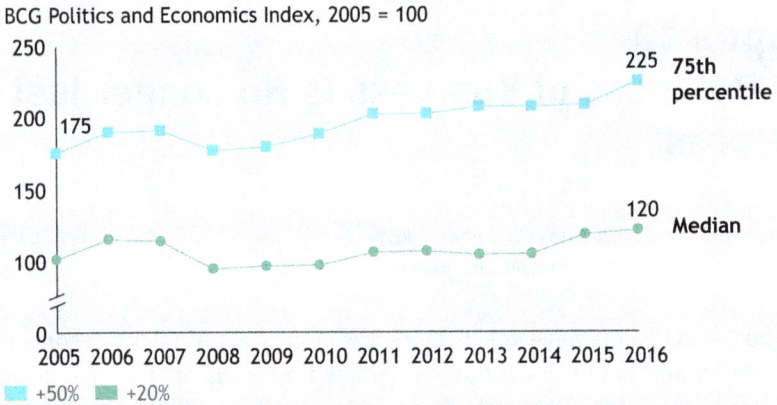

Note: The index captures the relative weight companies devote to discussing economic and political issues in their 10-K documents. The index is based on a natural language processing model using 10-K documents for 750 public companies from 2005 through 2016.
Source: BCG Henderson Institute.

Figure 10.1: Political and economic issues have become more important.

Does it matter? Our research shows that firms that are more exposed to political and economic feedback tend to have lower profit margins (see Figure 10.2).

AN INCREASE IN THE BCG POLITICS AND ECONOMICS INDEX LOWERS...

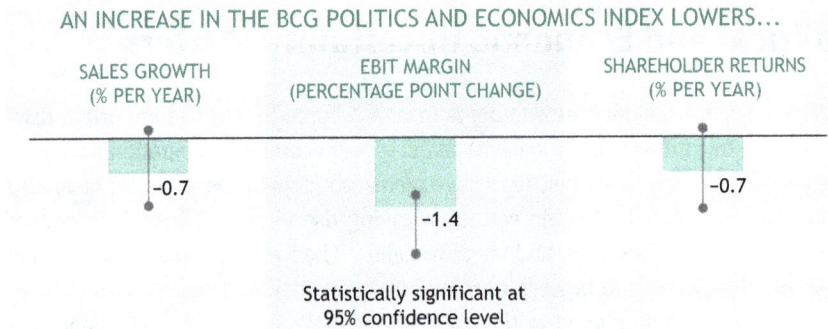

Note: The index captures the relative weight companies devote to discussing economic and political issues in their 10-K documents. The index is based on a natural language processing model using 10-K documents for 750 public companies from 2005 through 2016. Graph shows coefficients for a one standard deviation change and 95% confidence interval. Dependent variables lagged by five years.
Source: BCG Henderson Institute.

Figure 10.2: Exposure to political and economic feedback hurts profits.

This is not a surprise. Political and regulatory intervention and economic volatility do not generally help profits. But interestingly, the effects on growth and value creation are more ambiguous. Even in situations of high political and economic exposure, savvy leaders can mitigate negative effects and create competitive advantage.

The increasing interconnectedness of business, economic, and political spheres causes disturbances to spread more quickly. From the perspective of corporate leaders, that translates into increased change and systemic uncertainty, with tangible business consequences. The performance gap between winners and losers in all industries is already bigger than ever, and large companies in particular are struggling to find growth. As a result, companies are now dying sooner – the five-year mortality rate has risen from 5% in 1970 to around 32% today.[2]

A New Mental Model: From Chess to Matryoshka Dolls

To thrive in this new climate, leaders need a different mental model for business strategy. Instead of seeing it as a self-contained game of chess, leaders should perhaps visualize it as a Russian *matryoshka* doll, the endearing set of wooden figures that are stacked inside one another. Why? Business today is part of a nested set of so-called complex adaptive systems: interconnected, dynamic systems in which local perturbations can give rise to unpredictable global effects and vice versa. As a consequence, leaders need to be able to both grasp each level and master the art of playing on more than one level at a time.

What does such a nested set of systems look like in business? Companies are part of business ecosystems, which in turn are embedded in local and national economies, which are interwoven with societies. Changes at lower levels (within industries and between firms) influence higher levels, such as the economy and the political system, that in turn reshape the fates of the systems within them – namely, companies.

---

2 Reeves, M., and J. Harnoss (2015), "Don't Let Your Company Get Trapped by Success," hbr. org, November 19, 2015, https://hbr.org/2015/11/dont-let-your-company-get-trapped-by-suc cess; and Reeves, M., S. Levin, and D. Ueda (2016), "The Biology of Corporate Survival," *Harvard Business Review*, January–February 2016, https://www.bcg.com/publications/2016/strat egy-business-unit-strategy-biology-of-corporate-survival.

In more predictable times, there is a stable equilibrium between levels, permitting business to focus mainly on business considerations. Today, the opposite is true. Many business leaders tell us that political and economic considerations currently impact performance expectations more than purely competitive considerations do. It is impossible to run a business these days without at least considering what is happening on other levels.

Nested Complex Adaptive Systems in Practice

Take the US retail industry, for example. Encouraged by China's entry into the WTO in 2001, US retailers built tightly orchestrated supply chains across the globe, taking advantage of a new politically induced opportunity for global cost arbitrage. These sourcing and logistics decisions have had significant effects on economic, social, and political levels. A first direct result was the lowering of domestic prices for many household goods – in fact, this effect was so strong that the US Federal Reserve took it into account when deciding on interest rates. A more indirect result of these business decisions was the displacement of production activity in the US, leading to job losses, a new sense of social and economic insecurity, and ultimately a nativist political backlash against the trade policies.

These effects were complicated by technological advances, which increased factory productivity and further reduced manufacturing employment even as domestic manufacturing output increased. In recent years, US retailers have been trying to increase the weight of domestic sourcing. This comes late, possibly too late to preserve the current model of global economic arbitrage. A border tax, still under consideration in some US policy circles, could even undermine this game entirely by wiping out a majority of the industry's profits.[3]

Imperatives for Business Leaders

What should business leaders do now? Above all, they need to understand that focusing only on the narrow game of business has become a risky proposition.

---

3 Rose, J., and M. Reeves (2017), "Rethinking Your Supply Chain in an Era of Protectionism," hbr.org, March 22, 2017, https://www.bcg.com/publications/2017/lean-manufacturing-rethinking-supply-chain-era-protectionism.

They need new approaches for understanding, managing, and shaping the phenomena that arise from nested dynamic systems. Going forward, leaders should embrace five imperatives to expand their game and ensure that their companies thrive under more complex conditions.

1. Build multilevel scenario analysis skills. In this new environment, firms need to become more politically and economically astute. For that, they first need to develop political and economic analysis capabilities in order to understand what is happening in each layer and to model implications and strategic choices. This analysis should rely not just on textbook theory and point predictions but also on empirical evidence from analogous situations. Consider exchange rate risk. While textbook economics suggests that the depreciation of the British pound would increase prices (and lower demand) for imports, past experience with exchange rate adjustments shows that the effect on a particular company relative to competitors depends on many firm-specific factors. Leaders should then probe the effects of political and social shifts on their strategies.

Contingent thinking helps. This involves developing scenarios that are rich and broad enough to challenge the implicit assumptions behind strategies, investment plans, and initiatives. Ideally, scenario analysis is not a one-off (or annual) exercise but part of an ongoing examination of strategy. Leaders can use these scenarios to define signposts ("If we see events of type X, this validates belief Y"), build better antennae to pick up signals earlier ("If we see X, type X events are likely to occur soon"), and discuss conditional actions ("If we see X, then do Y"). This is easier said than done. Take European utility companies, for example, which – despite substantial political capacities and sophisticated scenario analysis skills – still struggled to grasp the impact of green energy preferences and policies on their business models.

2. Become more resilient. Given the inherent unpredictability of nested complex systems, not every adverse effect on business can be foreseen or mitigated. This means businesses need to become more resilient so that they can sustain and possibly even gain relative advantage from external shocks. Biological systems have evolved this quality over time. In our research, we found that organizations are more robust if they have three qualities of such systems: redundant elements (in their manufacturing network, for instance), internal diversity (such as in problem-solving approaches), and modularity (a network of loosely linked instead of tightly integrated parts). For example, when a fire destroyed the production lines of one of Toyota's key suppliers, the company was able to quickly activate and switch to other suppliers, avoiding assembly line interruptions that could have cost Toyota millions of dollars.

3. Shape the system. To moderate their exposure to uncertainty, large firms can strategically shape their immediate neighborhood to build safe havens of relative predictability. They can do so by controlling the context in which value is created or exchanged. Ecosystem formation (of suppliers and partners, for instance) is one such strategy, because it can allow the orchestrator to shape the context by establishing control over information flows and pricing mechanisms. Consider Amazon: By partnering with thousands of smaller independent e-commerce players, Amazon sees external shocks sooner, can percolate change within its own operations faster, and can adjust the degree of coupling between itself and players by changing the terms of exchange. It can also buffer itself against change by being agnostic to the product portfolio transacted on its platforms.

4. Recreate the narrative. In the long run, few things are as powerful as ideas. To get a better feel for the emergence of ideas that can spread and shape social and political layers, firms need to engage diverse audiences beyond their target customers and listen more closely to them. From that starting point, they should also aim to shape the discussion. Narratives, essentially storified ideas, are powerful because they can redefine what is legitimate and valuable. Take GE, for example. In a well-received and widely cited speech in 2016, CEO Jeff Immelt laid out a new vision[4] for the future of globalization and reiterated GE's commitment to building manufacturing centers and capabilities across the globe. In other words, GE is attempting to rewrite the narrative of globalization to address widening faults in the prevailing one.

5. Reframe leadership. Leaders need to continue focusing on value creation for customers and shareholders, but they must do so within new constraints created by economic and political layers in the broader system. To do so, leaders need to broaden their leadership repertoire. In particular, they need to increase their contribution as *antennae* that sense changing political and social signals and as *disruptors* that translate external change signals into organizational action and overcome organizational inertia. To shape the system and the narrative, leaders must balance the need for higher visibility into and influence

---

4 https://www.ge.com/news/reports/the-world-i-see-immelts advice-to-win-in-the-time-of-globalization.

on economic and political layers with a sense of humility about their own degree of control over desired outcomes.

Individuals, companies, economies, societies, and political systems are increasingly and inextricably connected, making it harder than ever to understand and steer individual firms in terms of business considerations alone. In times like these, the business of business requires more than just executing or thinking about business. To refresh their game, leaders should see their firms as embedded in interconnected, nested local and global systems. Leaders who understand and are able to maneuver in this new environment will position their companies to take advantage of these new complexities.

Martin Reeves, Georg Kell, Fabien Hassan
Chapter 11
The Case for Corporate Statesmanship

In a December 2017 interview, Volkswagen CEO Matthias Müller suggested that it is time to replace subsidies for diesel fueled vehicles with incentives that support electric vehicles. "I've become convinced that we should question the sense and purpose of the diesel subsidies," Müller told *Handelsblatt*. "If the switch to environmentally friendly e-cars is to succeed, diesel combustion engines can't continue to be subsidized the way they have been forever."

These words from a major diesel vehicle producer sparked a debate in the EU, where nearly half of all new cars sold run on diesel. This move could well trigger a transformational shift in the transportation industry.

The Volkswagen story is an example of corporate statesmanship. We believe that there is now a strong case for CEOs to take a bolder role in addressing some of society's major issues.

What is Corporate Statesmanship?

In politics, statesmanship refers to the skill of managing state affairs; a statesman, according to Merriam-Webster, is "a wise, skillful, and respected political leader." Statesmen place the common good above their own interests and actively work to shape the context.

Because they control wealth, the fate of employees, and the products they market, CEOs are influential political players, whether or not they realize or exercise their power. They can therefore realistically aspire to statesmanship by acting for the common good and not just the immediate interests of their companies.

We can define *corporate statesmanship* as the action of a company, and in particular of its CEO, to intervene in public affairs to foster collective action in support of the common good beyond the scope of his or her enlightened self-interest.

https://doi.org/10.1515/9783110775174-011

Society Faces Unprecedented Challenges

Social stresses abound, and CEOs faced a moment of truth in 2018,[1] especially in the US, where companies faced greater scrutiny because of tax reductions and regulatory relief. The societal challenges we face are well known. Inequalities have been strongly increasing over the past three decades, although more slowly in Europe than in the rest of the world (see Figure 11.1). The rise of a new protectionism is part of a backlash against globalization that is starting to impact business itself. The capacity of technology to foster progress and economic development is being questioned. The development of AI and robotization is increasingly feared as threats to employment rather than seen as drivers of opportunity.

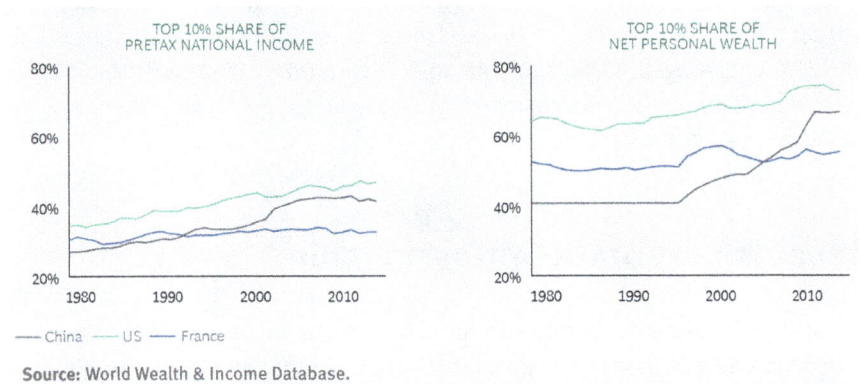

Source: World Wealth & Income Database.

Figure 11.1: Inequality has increased over the past three decades.

Another major challenge is the declining ability of the public sector to protect public goods – in particular the environment. The latest research[2] shows that despite the technologies at our disposal, we will likely miss the targets of the Paris climate accord. And a growing world population will place further stress on the environment: irreversible biodiversity losses, water scarcity, lack of arable land, and pressure on protected areas all seem likely to intensify.

Traditionally, we would expect governments to address these issues. In most of the world, there is a historic division of roles: corporations drive economic activity while governments take care of the common good.

---

1 https://www.linkedin.com/pulse/2018-moment-truth-ceos-rich-lesser-1/.
2 https://www.bcg.com/publications/2017/preparing-warmer-world.

As a result, there is an understandable reluctance for firms to get involved in public affairs. And giving companies a larger role can certainly create conflicts of interest, akin to having the fox watch the hen house. Numerous historical cases of failures of self-regulation support this view. Alan Greenspan, the former chairman of the Federal Reserve, famously claimed, "I made a mistake in presuming that the self-interest of organizations was such that they were best capable of protecting their own shareholders."

Governments Won't Necessarily Be Able to Address Challenges

There are good reasons to believe that governments may not be in a position to address some of today's challenges by themselves.

The scope and scale of some of the challenges are arguably too broad even for large countries, while weakening global cooperation reduces the chances for collective action. Political cycles limit the ability of governments to address long-term issues. On average, there are 1.7 national elections every quarter in the EU,[3] undermining the continuity needed to attack long-term challenges. And increasing political polarization further limits opportunities for public action in many parts of the world.

Financial pressures also contribute to institutional fragility and constrain public action. The welfare state is reaching its limits in developed countries, driven by an aging population and a shift from public wealth to private capital (see Figure 11.2).

The picture becomes even more complex if we consider the compounded effect of these challenges. For instance, 2015 research demonstrates the statistically significant effect of income inequality[4] on political polarization.

As a result of these and other factors, confidence in governmental institutions is falling, which further reduces the power of states as change agents. According to the Pew Research Center,[5] public trust in the government is near historic lows in the US. Only 18% of Americans today say they can trust the government to "do what is right."

---

3 https://voxeu.org/article/reducing-frequency-electoral-cycles-eu-proposal-synchronising-national-and-european-elections.

4 https://papers.ssrn.com/sol3/papers.cfm?abstract_id=2649215.

5 https://www.pewresearch.org/politics/2021/05/17/public-trust-in-government-1958-2021/.

NET PUBLIC AND PRIVATE WEALTH
(% OF NATIONAL INCOME)

Private wealth

Public wealth[1]

—— US —— UK —— France —— Germany —— Spain

Sources: World Wealth & Income Database; *Financial Times.*
[1]Not marked to market, but the trend is clear.

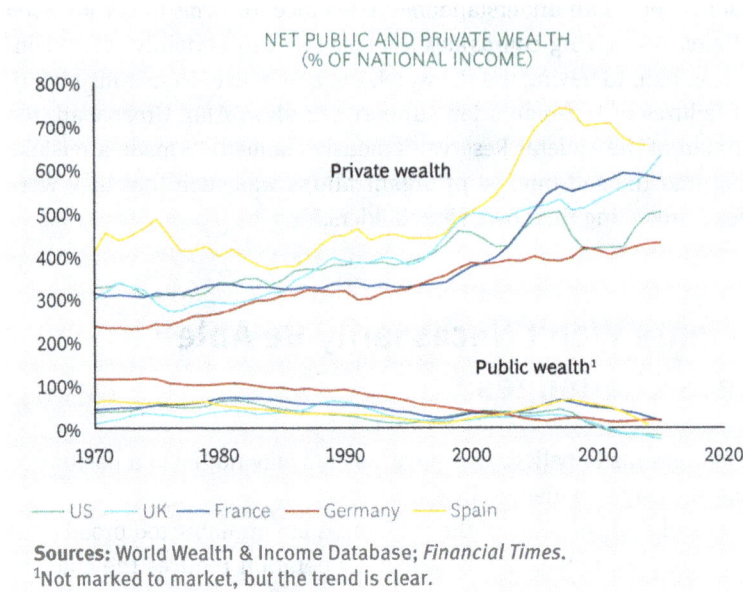

Figure 11.2: Public wealth is declining in developed countries.

The Case for Stepping Up

Given this, there is a strong case for corporations to step up their statesmanship.

Of course, many CEOs fear that a more public role might expose them to backlash, especially in a context of increasing skepticism toward institutions. In a recent survey,[6] while 38% responded that CEOs have a responsibility to speak out on controversial issues, 36% said they believe the top reason for CEO activism is "to get media attention."

As in postwar Japan, corporations are economic giants but still political dwarfs. Leaders tend to focus on immediate business problems: A 2017 survey by the National Association of Corporate Directors showed that only 2% of board directors see the role of business in society as having the greatest effect on their company over the next 12 months.

---

6 https://hbr.org/2016/06/is-it-safe-for-ceos-to-voice-strong-political-opinions.

However, the risk of action needs to be balanced against the risk of inaction. If companies remain passive,[7] they could soon find themselves damaged by an environment of escalating political risk.

Ultimately, consumers and society have the power to sanction or restrict the freedom of action of global corporations. Regardless of political inclinations, corporate leaders have a common interest in preserving the game of business and defending the drivers of growth, like technology and globalization.

Corporations don't just have a self-interest to step up – they are also well positioned to do so. Fundamentally, they are effective at problem solving. They can act globally, in contrast to national governments. They have access to resources, skills, and technology. Profits and cash accumulation are at historical highs, especially in the United States, in light of recent corporate tax reform; so there is a large margin for action right now. As the influence of business has grown, so has its ability to shape the provision of the public goods that are essential for market stability.

Ultimately, business cannot succeed if societies fail. Global markets need global rules for business to play its proper role in creating wealth and spreading solutions.

Statesmanship Is More than Corporate Responsibility

The business community is increasingly stepping up on sustainability and corporate responsibility (CR), not least because of growing evidence[8] of a positive link with financial performance. The recent ascendancy of sustainable investing, enabled with tools such as the Arabesque S-Ray, will further accelerate good practices across industries. This alignment of finance with CR could make a significant contribution to society in terms of environmental stewardship, workplace conditions, and good governance.

In essence, CR is a long-term maximization of self-interest in which companies ensure that they don't damage themselves by undermining their own environments. CR is fundamentally about individual action in ways that are

---

7 https://www.bcg.com/publications/2016/strategy-globalization-saving-globalization-technology-from-themselves.
8 https://www.bcg.com/publications/2017/total-societal-impact-new-lens-strategy.

compatible with common interest – in other words, "doing well by doing good" within an existing policy framework.

Statesmanship, by contrast, goes a step further. It is about shaping the policy framework to advance public and private interests and changing the game by influencing the collective will (see Figure 11.3). It tackles problems that can't be resolved through the enlightened self-interest of individual companies. In economics, the prisoner's dilemma describes situations in which without collective action all actors tend to undermine one another, which leads to suboptimal individual outcomes. In other words, because each company follows its own path, an entire industry or economy ends up hurting itself. In those cases, statesmen are needed to foster cooperation and lift everyone to a better equilibrium by changing the nature of the game.

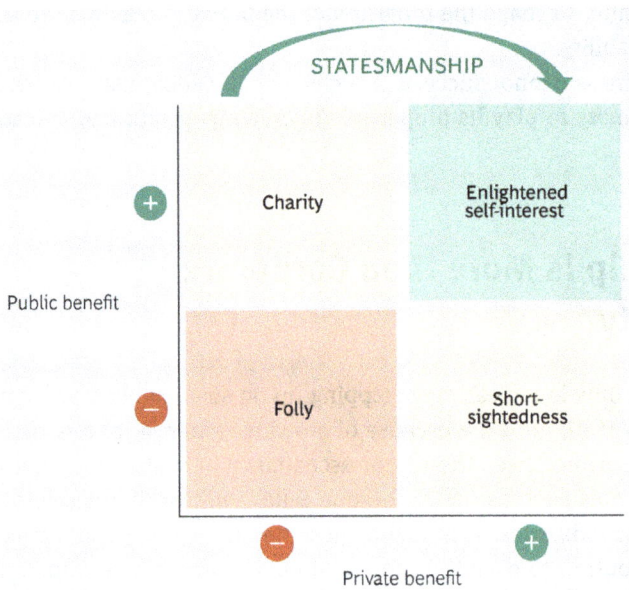

Source: BCG Henderson Institute.

Figure 11.3: Statesmanship can shape collective benefit.

Cybersecurity is a good example of a prisoner's dilemma in business. Everybody has a direct interest in protecting their data: citizens, consumers, and producers alike. But nobody has an interest in investing too much in the security of their own systems. This leads to systemic vulnerability, where breaches of security could have a negative impact on all and take down companies.

The Path to Statesmanship

First, Be a Good Citizen

A good statesman must be a good citizen. Gaining trust requires behaving responsibly and being perceived in this light by other stakeholders. Maximization of total shareholder return (TSR) within legal boundaries is not enough. Leaders need to clearly define a human purpose,[9] the higher social goal their corporation serves, and ensure that their impact is compatible with that purpose. And they need to ensure that their own operations are based on values and a commitment to integrity.

A good start is the assessment of a firm's economic, social, environmental, and political impact. To this end, companies can think in terms of their total societal impact (TSI),[10] a collection of measures and assessments that can be used to lay the foundations for a sound sustainability strategy.

Understand and Protect the Rules of the Game

Above being a good citizen, statesmen need to protect the rules and institutions that guarantee balance in society. Companies benefit from a "license to operate" from society. Statesmen understand the underlying conditions of the game and the lines that cannot be crossed without jeopardizing that license.

Consider Allergan CEO Brent Saunders: "The health care industry has had a long-standing unwritten social contract with patients, physicians, policy makers and the public at large," he wrote in a company blog. The perceived breach of that contract could threaten the entire industry. "As the focus on price has heated up," he noted, "the innovation ecosystem has come under assault, and it is fragile."

To protect the game, Allergan offered a new "social contract" to patients, with a focus on responsible pricing. The company then argued for industry-wide action, along with other CEOs. Recent data suggests Allergan's commitment on pricing may be shaping industry norms.

---

9 https://www.bcg.com/publications/2018/humanization-corporation.
10 https://www.bcg.com/publications/2017/total-societal-impact-new-lens-strategy.

Bolster Government

To play the game of business, companies need a fair set of rules and a referee. We tend to forget the value of regulation and criticize overregulation, but the rule of law is a basic condition for economic development. In Africa, fintech CEOs have been calling for regulatory action to prevent fraud and facilitate the development of the industry. As SimbaPay CEO Nyasinga Onyancha has noted, "Regulations have a huge role to play in ensuring the fintech industry becomes bigger and better."

In developed economies, too, companies should support the role of the state as regulator and referee. Elon Musk's letter[11] calling for the banning of autonomous weapons, which select and engage targets without human intervention, is an example of embracing regulation for social good. As the letter states, this about protecting the game and preventing "a major public backlash against AI that curtails its future societal benefits."

Support Smart Regulation

Empowering governments is a first step, but corporate leaders also need to propose and support smart regulations to preserve social balance. A case in point is the financial industry, which is highly complex and interconnected. It shares many features with biological systems,[12] in which all actors benefit from the ecosystem. In such situations, actors that overstretch the system by systematically maximizing their private benefits may provoke its collapse.

Because statesmen are aware of those dynamics, they assume a wider responsibility and support regulations that underpin a sustainable future for their industry. ExxonMobil CEO Darren Woods realizes that "growing demand creates a dual challenge: providing energy to meet people's needs while managing the risks of climate change." Therefore, in his first blog post as CEO, he advocated a "uniform price of carbon applied consistently across the economy" as the smartest way to meet that dual challenge.

---

11 https://www.theguardian.com/technology/2017/aug/20/elon-musk-killer-robots-experts-outright-ban-lethal-autonomous-weapons-war.
12 https://www.pnas.org/content/pnas/112/41/12543.full.pdf.

Oppose Injustice

When confronted with situations that are obviously unfair, the statesman takes action. As Elie Wiesel put it, "We must take sides. Neutrality helps the oppressor, never the victim." Assessments of "right" and "wrong" should be informed by universal values and principles that we have learned from history.

According to the framework developed by economist Albert O. Hirschman, there are three ways to act: Exit (refraining from participating in markets that don't meet certain standards), Voice (protesting publicly), and Loyalty (silently approving where general interest prevails, but the silence is chosen rather than by default; the decision can be explained later if necessary).

"Voice" may generate unwanted exposure for a corporation. One option for CEOs to mitigate such a risk is to distinguish their opinions as citizens from those of their companies. Sergey Brin attended demonstrations in his personal capacity, not as the president of Google. This can be a good way to respond without the company appearing to customers and stakeholders as politically biased.

Take the Lead

The major issues of society are well known. Sometimes even the solutions are obvious, but political, social, or economic conditions prevent those solutions from being implemented. Statesmen do not use this as an excuse and instead take the lead and demonstrate that action is possible.

In the cybersecurity example above, Google built a group of hackers called Project Zero in order to identify and address digital threats, with a focus on the software made by other companies. This is a tangible way for Google to show that it takes responsibility for the overall stability of the system.

Shape and Join Horizontal Coalitions with Other Companies

Taking the lead is meant to trigger collective action. For businesses, the rationale for engaging with others is not just about maximizing impact. Acting with other industry players is also a way to ensure that the conditions of competition remain fair and equivalent for all.

CEOs can help form and shape such coalitions to realize their values. There are many ways to do this, but the UN Global Compact has been decisive in providing a unified framework for business coalitions across a wide array of sustainability principles based on universal values.

In a particularly striking example, more than 400 companies, including Microsoft, Adidas, and Sony, have committed to being climate neutral[13] – that is, to minimize their greenhouse gas emissions and compensate for unavoidable emissions. Businesses should not be afraid to engage with other types of actors too: the climate coalition also includes individuals, cities, and nonprofits.

Shape Vertical Coalitions with Investors

CEOs have a direct legal responsibility to their shareholders. Business leaders often use this as an argument for remaining within the strict limits of their assumed mandates and focusing on the maximization of TSR. However, there are now many examples of investors pressuring leaders to take a stand on societal issues. In January 2018, two Apple investors pressured the company to address concerns over smartphone addiction. They requested that management better assess the mental health effects on children and take appropriate action.

Neglecting this type of pressure might come at a high price. Norway's pension fund, the world's largest sovereign wealth fund, which owns on average 1.3% of every single listed company on earth, decided to divest from oil and gas[14] as part of a climate change strategy.

Sustainable investing enabled by technology and big data analysis, as advanced by firms like Arabesque, is turning investors into increasingly powerful allies for corporate statesmen in addressing social challenges.

Build Narratives

It is often impossible for even informed citizens to know all the facts of a subject – which are in many cases often disputed – especially in the case of controversial social issues. People understand reality individually and collectively through stories. Statesmen exert influence and shape minds and foster action

---

13 https://unfccc.int/climate-action/climate-neutral-now/measure-your-emissions.
14 https://www.ft.com/content/611c2e9e-cad9-11e7-aa33-c63fdc9b8c6c.

through narratives. CEOs need to explain why they believe what they believe and advocate for it by building understandable and compelling narratives, which not only stand up to scrutiny but can create alignment and support.

Lyft cofounder John Zimmer is well aware of a risk of backlash against new forms of mobility. So he argues that car sharing is more than a business – it has a huge impact on the design of cities. As he wrote on Medium, it has "tremendous implications on global economics, health, social equality, the environment, and overall quality of life." This puts the company in a better position to shape the future of the industry.

Business leaders need to face the inconvenient truth that some aspects of collective welfare can't come from individual maximization efforts, even enlightened ones. They require the "technology of leadership" to solve the prisoner's dilemma of noncooperation leading to poorer outcomes for all.

Corporations that lead will be trusted more and accepted as partners by governments and citizens as actions will foster more actions.

Andrew Cainey
Chapter 12
Mind the Gap: Navigating the New Fault Lines of Global Business

Long the beneficiaries of a stable geopolitical environment and liberalizing trade flows, multinationals now face a more uncertain, challenging world. National security and differences in values are back on the political agenda with a vengeance. Governments increasingly address commercial questions through the lens of national security and values, not just of economics. Across borders, there is more volatility, antagonism, and uncertainty. Fault lines are opening up in the global economy.

Day to day, companies now face the risk of sudden export or import bans on key suppliers and customers – sometimes for clear reasons, sometimes not. They may find acquisition or investor opportunities blocked or subject to lengthy reviews. They may need to decide how to comply with contradictory laws, originating from US and China with extraterritorial reach. And they may need to justify to stakeholders in one country why they continue to operate in another. How then can multinationals, with business models built on operating across borders, navigate these new global fault lines?

The Forces Underlying the New Geopolitics

Two major underlying factors are at work:

First, national differences are coming to the fore, as economic power shifts to higher-growth economies in Asia, in particular to China, and rivalry takes the place of engagement and cooperation.

China, now the world's second-largest economy, is choosing a more assertive role, more explicitly pursuing its own interests as it sees fit. As China integrated into the world economy, some western leaders simply assumed a convergence toward western models of market economics and governance. In 2000, President Bill Clinton described China's WTO accession as "agreeing to import one of democracy's most cherished values: economic freedom" and said that "the genie of freedom will not go back into the bottle."[1] In 1999, then-presidential candidate

---

1 https://macropolo.org/analysis/china-us-engagement-policy/.

https://doi.org/10.1515/9783110775174-012

George W. Bush stated: "Economic freedom creates the habits of liberty, and habits of liberty create the expectations of democracy . . . Trade freely with China and time is on our side."[2]

Instead, under President Xi, the Chinese Communist Party has returned to prominence across all aspects of life: "Party, government, military, civilian, and academic, east, west, south, north and center, the Party leads everything."[3] The emphasis is on the "Great Rejuvenation of the Chinese Nation" and on national security against internal and external threats. This "big security" is defined expansively across 11 categories: political, territorial, military, economic, cultural, social, ecological, science and technology, information, nuclear, and natural resources.[4]

On the international stage, Robert Zoellick, then-US Deputy Secretary of State, urged China in 2005 to become a "responsible stakeholder" in the global system. But this did not consider how China might wish to reshape such a system. In fact, rather than accepting or rejecting the western-developed multilateral system, China seeks to contribute, adapt, and supplement it based on its own position.

In parallel, under President Trump, the US began to judge its interests best-served by less multilateral engagement in general and a more confrontational approach with China. The US sees China's growing technological and military capabilities as a competitive challenge and a source of at least some of America's own economic problems: One analysis estimated the US employment impact of the low-cost manufacturing "China Shock" at 2.4 million jobs.[5] The US government has also criticized China for its "economic aggression" and "state-sponsored intellectual property theft."[6] The US-China relationship is now framed primarily as a "strategic competition."[7] The open question is how wide-ranging, intense, and dangerous this competition will be. Is it a New Cold War?

Political concerns about globalization go wider than the US and China. Governments now see the risks more than the rewards of interdependence. Whereas before, voters saw the benefits of lower-priced manufactured imports and increased international travel, many now pay more attention to lost manufacturing

---

2 Schell, O. (2020), "The Death of Engagement," *The Wire China*, https://docs.house.gov/meetings/IG/IG00/20200701/110846/HHRG-116-IG00-Wstate-SchellO-20200701.pdf.
3 https://www.reuters.com/article/us-china-congress-maoists-idUSKBN1CX005.
4 https://www.chinausfocus.com/peace-security/framing-chinas-national-security.
5 https://www.nber.org/papers/w21906.
6 https://www.whitehouse.gov/wp-content/uploads/2018/06/FINAL-China-Technology-Report-6.18.18-PDF.pdf.
7 https://trumpwhitehouse.archives.gov/wp-content/uploads/2020/05/U.S.-Strategic-Approach-to-The-Peoples-Republic-of-China-Report-5.24v1.pdf.

jobs at home, fears of uncontrolled immigration and the risk of other countries withholding their vital supplies in times of need. Leaders from India to Europe to Brazil speak more vocally of national identity and values. Ideology is back in the discourse.

Second, the all-pervasive role of technology and data has changed the nature of security risk. Technology is increasingly "dual-use," with both civilian and military applications, making it a challenge to split economic considerations from national security. It makes broad swathes of national infrastructure vulnerable to remote disruption through technology networks. The UK government identifies thirteen areas of Critical National Infrastructure requiring protection, including Energy, Finance, Transport, and Water.

Technology also raises new ethical questions in areas such as AI and facial recognition. Countries are developing, deploying, and regulating these in markedly different ways, especially in the area of surveillance. And, ultimately, economic prosperity underpins national security – which requires leadership in key technologies. China identified ten such industries for investment in its Made in China 2025 initiative.

Taken together, these two changes point to a world where countries each take a more integrated view of security, economics, and values at the national level, while diverging in important ways at the international level. "Strategic autonomy" is favored over interdependence. These fundamentals will not change easily or quickly regardless of who leads a country. Where leaders do make a difference is in their choices about what to do and how to do it. Alongside this, the faltering multilateral system or "rules-based order" makes tensions worse and uncertainty greater. Much needs updating – to reflect shifts in economic power and to establish "rules of the game" in fast-changing areas such as technology and the environment. This calls for leaders to build the coalitions needed to do this. But whose rules? Whose order?

One World: How Many Systems?

Are we heading, as some propose, to "One World, Two Systems"? This ill-defined phrase harkens back to a Cold War world split between NATO and the Soviet Bloc. China's development of a distinct internet ecosystem behind the "Great Firewall" is called into evidence. Will the world divide again into "spheres of influence," operating on different technology standards and trading rules?

Such a clean split is highly unlikely. Countries, like companies, want to avoid choosing sides, maintain options, and pursue their own agenda. Even the Cold War saw the founding of the Non-Aligned Movement of nations.

Relationships between countries are complex and many-dimensioned, not binary. Recall that, prior to 3G, Korea, Japan, the US, and Europe operated on incompatible mobile phone standards. Today the choice for 5G is between different suppliers on the same standard. Australia, Japan, Singapore, Vietnam, and others have now signed two, partly overlapping, free trade agreements, the CPTPP[8] and the RCEP.[9] One includes China and one does not – at least currently. The US is in neither.

A more likely future is a world will be made of up of multiple groupings, with overlapping members and different groups focused on different purposes, such as security, technology, and trade, and with different geographical reach. This is not a binary "decoupled world," but rather a different world, adjusting to change as explored in the BCG paper "Is Decoupling Bad?"[10] In some areas – health pandemic monitoring may be one – the benefits of a single common approach will justify compromises between countries, whatever their differences. In others, a smaller group of countries will agree to closer alignment. The European Union stands out here. New initiatives are still taking shape, such as the Quad[11] and D-10,[12] a would-be grouping of ten democracies that the UK has proposed.

Companies will need to keep navigating tensions, contradictions, and opportunities in the relations between countries. The choices that national leaders make will matter as much as the underlying economic and technological forces.

---

8 The Comprehensive and Progressive Agreement for Trans-Pacific Partnership: Australia, Brunei, Canada, Chile, Japan, Malaysia, Mexico, New Zealand, Peru, Singapore, and Vietnam.
9 The Regional Comprehensive Economic Partnership: Australia, Brunei, Cambodia, China, Indonesia, Japan, Laos, Malaysia, Myanmar, New Zealand, the Philippines, Singapore, South Korea, Thailand, and Vietnam.
10 https://bcghendersoninstitute.com/is-decoupling-bad-1fd836d3c913.
11 Quad: Australia, India, Japan, and the US.
12 D-10: G-7 economies (Canada, France, Germany, Italy, Japan, the United Kingdom, and the United States) plus Australia, India, and South Korea.

Beyond the Headlines: Understanding the Political Dynamics

It is not yet clear what will replace the stability and structure of the post-Cold War order. To see beyond the noise of day-to-day headlines, companies should consider three dimensions of international relations for insight into how the political dynamics and key bilateral relationships are developing:

1. Autonomy vs. Interdependence: How do national government leaders see the balance between costs and benefits and between autonomy and interdependence in their foreign policy? And in regard to which countries? US-China relations, of course, stand out. But so too do India's relations with China, the US, and Japan; as well as the EU-US relationship, given an EU focus on "strategic autonomy."

2. Antagonism vs. Acceptance: Do national leaders share some form of mutual understanding about the interests of each country? Or is the situation inherently zero-sum with a reluctance or inability to reconcile contradictory positions? Examples include the US-China military power balance in Pacific and differing positions on human rights. But also include, more directly for business, disparate trade practices and technology competition.

3. Volatility vs. Stability: How consistent is the focus and level of antagonism or acceptance between countries? Recently, there has been more volatility on both the US and Chinese sides, with emotional rhetoric often not followed by consistent policy actions. Stability reduces the risk of misunderstanding and helps long-term planning.

Geopolitical fault-lines open up where leaders push for significantly more autonomy from the other. They are deepest and most harmful where the antagonism and volatility is the greatest. They also tend to be self-reinforcing. Following the US bans on certain semiconductor exports to China, China is redoubling its efforts to build its own capabilities, vindicated in its assessment that dependence on the US was a risk.

Seasoned observers argue that strategic competition between the US and China is inevitable on multiple fronts. But leaders can act to agree rules and guard-rails for this competition. They can move, as former Australian Prime Minister Kevin Rudd articulates, from unmanaged to managed strategic competition.[13] They can also agree to cooperate on global issues such as the environment and health, and to update and adapt multilateral rules of engagement to today's world. Fu Ying, a former Vice-Minister of Foreign Affairs of China, argues that the key issue is whether the US and China are able to objectively judge each other's strengths and purposes, and find a middle ground where their respective goals won't be mutually exclusive.[14] This will make the difference between "zero-sum confrontation" and "co-opetition."

All this takes time, effort, and focus but offers the prospect of reduced antagonism and increased stability. It may in time reduce the impetus for autonomy – but differing interests will remain and so will the fault-lines.

Which Business Sectors are Most Affected?

A nation-based, security-and-values perspective has understandably long dominated sectors such as defense and aerospace. It has also played a role in energy, resources, and some defined areas of technology. But now dating apps, face masks, and lobsters get attention, too. Does geopolitics now affect *every* sector?

Data collection from a country's citizens is increasingly viewed from a national security perspective. The US blocked the acquisition of Grindr, a gay dating app, by a Chinese company on the grounds of preventing Chinese access to sensitive data. In addition, the Trump administration questioned whether Chinese fintech companies such as Alipay pose risks. As every business becomes a "data business," where do countries draw the line on security? And when is a security risk assessment really cover for protectionism or sheer anti-foreign bias?

The COVID-19 pandemic highlighted China's dominant role in the global manufacturing of face masks. While Chinese production and exports grew rapidly to meet demand, countries see now a dependency risk and aim to build their own manufacturing capacity. In which sectors does it make sense to pay to build up self-sufficiency rather than buy from the lowest-price supply source? And who will pay?

One analysis identified 56% of EU exports to China as "completely benign," free of any security implications and placed 83% of Chinese imports into the EU

---

13 https://www.kevinrudd.com/archive/2020-07-09-the-us-china-relationship-needs-a-new-organising-principle.
14 https://www.chinausfocus.com/foreign-policy/after-the-pandemic-then-what.

in the same category.[15] But when tensions rise and fault-lines between countries deepen everything becomes fair game – anything can be deemed a risk.

Individual businesses can fall victim to broader tensions in bilateral relationships. In 2017, China banned packaged tour groups to South Korea in response to the basing there of US THAAD missiles. One year later, the ban was lifted as relations thawed. As China's relations with Australia hit a low, China introduced new inspections of lobster imports, to address potential health risks, that effectively blocked the imports. The UK's new National Security and Investment Bill proposes mandatory review of acquisitions by foreign acquirers in sectors as broad as transport, AI, and critical suppliers to government. However tightly worded the legislation, what affects national security is ultimately open to political interpretation, based on the geopolitical environment.

Geopolitical risk for companies is now pervasive, beyond neatly segregated industry categories. Technology and data are part of the reason, but risk can flare up suddenly when international relations become tense, whatever the business.

What Should Companies Do?

In this changed and changing world, companies need to determine how geopolitics affects their own business. A world of greater autonomy and likely continued antagonism places a premium on companies being good corporate citizens in each country. But, when fault-lines between countries deepen, it is the cross-border challenges that become greater, causing tensions internally and with stakeholders. HSBC bank received extensive parliamentary criticism in the UK for its public support of the Hong Kong National Security Law. Google's US employees were reportedly disturbed by Google's plan, "Isolated Region," to provide ring-fenced cloud services in China's controlled internet environment. In extreme cases of war, multinationals have had to split operations as Coca Cola did in Germany during World War II.

Companies need to consider action in six areas:

1. Assess and monitor the risks on an ongoing basis. In each country where they operate, companies need to assess the security risks and questions of value potentially associated with their business. In some situations, assessing risk to

---

15 Kratz, A., M. Mingey, and D.H. Rosen (2020), "Exploring a Green List for EU-China Economic Relations," *Rhodium Group*, https://rhg.com/research/green-list/.

individual employees is also important. The greater challenge comes for multinationals that straddle geopolitical fault lines – or are at risk from sudden changes in where those fault lines lie. They need first to assess which fault lines are most relevant; how deep and fixed they are; where they cut across the business; and what new ones may emerge. The perspective to take is that of a skeptical outsider or a determined competitor, seeking to stretch these arguments for competitive advantage. Companies need to invest in enhanced monitoring of the geopolitical environment and identify where contingency planning makes sense in the face of uncertainty.

2. Be an even better corporate citizen in each country. Foreign multinationals have long committed to making a "second home" in major markets such as China. Now is the time to double down on these efforts. Government relations and compliance functions may need upgrading. Look also to demonstrate how multinational operations bring local value to a country.

3. Consider where separation makes sense. By increasing operational separation between countries, organizational changes can help address external perceptions of risk and foreign control. Changes to governance and ownership structures, additional local stock market listings and internal reorganization may each have a role. The argument for localizing production and supply chains strengthens. Strong local talent, with the corporate credibility to decide locally, while remaining consistent with global principles, becomes more important. In the most extreme cases, spinning off a country operation completely may be the solution.

4. Determine whether growth opportunities have shifted. Growth across fault lines has become tougher. Acquisition opportunities may dry up. Companies in a start-up phase or a weaker competitive position may find the best exit route.

5. Look for the opportunities from geopolitical risk. Change brings opportunity. Companies may benefit from shifting competitive dynamics as a company's national identity becomes a factor in some purchasing decisions. Industrial policy for key technologies and domestic manufacturing is back on the agenda in the US and Europe – a response to China's own policies. The Japanese government is offering subsidies to relocate manufacturing from China back to home and to other countries. Companies need to assess the durability of such policy changes and whether they change the calculus on where and how to invest. Competitively, dynamics can also shift.

6. Be a force for good in shaping the context. Companies have the opportunity to lead and help address geopolitical challenges through acts of corporate statesmanship. BCG defines corporate statesmanship as "the action of a company, and in particular of its CEO, to intervene in public affairs to foster collective action in support of the common good beyond the scope of his or her enlightened self-interest."[16] For some, in sensitive commercial situations, keeping one's head down may be the right solution. But multinationals have benefited greatly from a stable, multilateral rules-based order. Especially in the areas of trade and investment, they are well-placed to contribute to the evolution of this multilateral system, as it adapts to new challenges in environment and technology and the shifting role of countries within the world economy. They can connect and bring people together across borders, find commonalities in what appear to be differences of values, and propose practical solutions to address sometimes-misplaced fears of security risk such as in the area of data and technology transfer. This can both strengthen a company's competitive edge and contribute to the common good.

---

16 https://www.bcg.com/en-us/publications/2018/case-corporate-statesmanship.

Martin Reeves, Roselinde Torres

Chapter 13
In Sync: Unlocking Collective Action in a Connected World

You didn't see me on television, you didn't see news stories about me. The kind of role that I tried to play was to pick up pieces or put together pieces out of which I hoped organization might come.
— Ella Baker

Civil rights leader Ella Baker was famous for eschewing monolithic top-down approaches, preferring to work behind the scenes to effect change, building on or combining existing efforts and engaging with the broadest set of stakeholders. To mobilize the vote, for example, she prodded civil rights activists to go beyond inspirational speeches and assemble all the "pieces" required, such as voter identification, education, and transportation.

Organizations (civil and commercial alike) frequently struggle against internal and external inertia, complexity, distraction, and fractiousness to get things done. Civil society often looks to business as a paragon of discipline – with its emphasis on goals, measurement, efficiency, and accountability – for lessons in how to effect action. But for today's complex, dynamic, multi-stakeholder problems, business also has much to learn from social activism.

Multi-dimensional matrix structures, excessive layers, complex procedures, competing agendas, and internal politics can all wreck the execution of apparently robust plans. Indeed, an explicit objective of many organizational transformation programs is to remove such barriers to nimble execution. But merely removing barriers to action is not enough to bring about change – as anyone who has witnessed the failure of a high-profile initiative can attest. In large organizations and societies, enacting change requires many people to synchronize new beliefs and behaviors. Because it is difficult to know what will motivate diverse individuals to act differently, and to predict the collective result when they do so, traditional linear approaches to change often fail.

In theory, digital technology should make things easier by increasing the reach, speed, and ease of communication. In practice, however, we observe the same failures of collective action in digital contexts. With business and societal challenges increasing the need for synchronized change,[1] it is important for

---

1 https://www.bcg.com/en-us/publications/2019/science-organizational-change.

https://doi.org/10.1515/9783110775174-013

leaders to understand how to make collective action work in an increasingly connected world.

The Limits of Project Management

Traditional project management applies a "classical" approach[2] to problem-solving. Large problems are divided into smaller ones, on the assumption that the sum of the solutions to each part will constitute an overall fix. These smaller problems are solved by collecting pertinent facts, analyzing root causes, identifying logical solutions, and encapsulating them in durable plans. The main challenges then become removing obstacles to change (such as complex processes or structures) and managing implementation in a disciplined fashion. This is done by setting clear, quantifiable goals; creating plans that cascade down to specific actions; assigning organizational accountability for each part of the plan; and tracking implementation and impact using key performance metrics.

This familiar approach is well-suited for challenges that can be decomposed, solved analytically, and executed within a single organization – such as streamlining a production process, reducing costs, or reorganizing. However, many problems are more complex,[3] such as those involving changing contexts, having interdependencies between different elements, diverse agents, or reaching beyond the boundaries of an organization.

Problems are often not decomposable: if we break them down and solve for each part, the result may not constitute an overall solution. And they are often not analytically tractable, because in a complex system, any one action potentially changes other agents' perceptions and actions. As a result, interventions cannot be boiled down to a simple unchanging set of instructions. Furthermore, even if we could identify the ideal solution, merely broadcasting it to participants might not motivate them to act or do so in a coordinated and effective manner. This problem is exacerbated when coordination must extend beyond a single organization and influence and control are diluted. For example, we know that reducing carbon emissions is required to slow or reverse global warming, and we know with some precision what each country, industry and individual would need to do to achieve this, yet we are still seemingly unable to mobilize collective

2 https://www.amazon.com/Your-Strategy-Needs-Execute-Approach/dp/1625275862/ref=sr_1_ 2?dchild=1&keywords=your+strategy+needs+a+strategy&qid=1596213143&sr=8-2.
3 https://www.bcg.com/publications/2020/resilience-more-important-than-efficiency.

action.[4] (Paradoxically, our biggest success in reducing emissions to date has been as an unintended side effect of dealing with COVID-19.)

Therefore, we need to broaden our approach beyond traditional project management. To do so, we need to look to other domains where *collective* action is required – such as social activism.

Requirements for Effective Collective Action

Sociologist Charles Tilly proposed that to be effective, a social movement must exhibit four key characteristics: its proponents must see the cause as **Worthy**, they must be **United** in their stance, they must be sufficiently **Numerous** make a difference, and they must be **Committed** to making change happen.[5] To this, others have added that the proponents must have sufficient **Diversity** for the cause to be of broad appeal.[6] This is not the only framework for looking at collective action, but it has the merits of being easily applicable, focusing on the social dimension of action, going beyond narrow economic considerations, and being readily applicable to both corporate and broader social contexts.

The framework immediately helps us understand some ways in which collective change initiatives often fail:

Failures of Worthiness

A cause must be seen as worthwhile by those who would join it, but perceived worthiness can be undermined in several ways.

-   *Triviality*: If an initiative is seen as insignificant in comparison to other competing causes or to individual aspirations, it is unlikely to create engagement. In business parlance, the ultimate *purpose* of the cause must be articulated, not just the actions associated with it. Today's employees increasingly seek not only economic security but also personal meaning in work, so if an initiative does not contribute to the greater good or help

---

4 https://bcghendersoninstitute.com/embracing-the-complexity-of-climate-change-64b0c58c1f41.

5 Tilly, Charles (2004). *Social movements, 1768–2004*, Paradigm Publishers.

6 Wouters, R., and S. Walgrave (2017). "What Makes Protest Powerful? Reintroducing and Elaborating Charles Tilly's WUNC Concept," https://www.researchgate.net/publication/313179891_WHAT_MAKES_PROTEST_POWERFUL_REINTRODUCING_AND_ELABORATING_CHARLES_TILLY'S_WUNC_CONCEPT.

them realize personal aspirations and values – or if this deeper purpose is not articulated clearly – it will not be compelling. For example, a cost-cutting effort may not be seen as worthwhile unless it is paired with a clear vision of how it will help serve the firm's economic and social purpose.

- *Instrumentalism*: Almost every issue in business today has some political aspect, which means that intentions will be closely scrutinized. If a cause is perceived as being merely a convenient pretext for personal gain or some other ulterior motive, then it is unlikely to gather support. In a corporate context, people can be compelled to act through hierarchical authority, but grudging compliance will likely not create lasting commitment or effective change. Furthermore, corporations increasingly need to deploy influence beyond the boundaries of the corporation to shape their economic and social context. Moreover, one should expect that messages may be deliberately coopted and distorted by others, requiring constant reiteration and clarification. As former president of Colombia, Juan Manuel Santos, confided in us, "Although we were ultimately successful, one of our major missteps in driving the peace process was hesitancy in reiterating our message, and naiveté in underestimating the extent to which it would be deliberately distorted by others."

Failures of Unity

If proponents do not speak and act in unity, they may send mixed messages and undermine the ability to gain support from a wider constituency.

- *Private inconsistency*: In public, leaders will usually manage to present a united front, but the true degree of unity will be judged from private interactions. Confiding dissenting opinions to others in private may establish individual trust, but it comes at the expense of public trust in an initiative. Duplicity can undermine an initiative from the outset, although this may not be obvious from official discussions and representations.
- *Misaligned mental models*: Members of a successful cause need to be committed not only to a course of action, but also to a common purpose and a common mental model of how intended actions will result in desired change. Otherwise, the cause is susceptible to "working in practice but not in theory," as Ben Bernanke famously quipped. This may not seem like a problem at first, but over time it is likely that new actions will be required as new challenges emerge – testing unity at this deeper level. This raises what philosophers call the intersubjectivity problem – how do I know that you are thinking what I am thinking? – and it can be addressed by being explicit and

precise about mental models, goals, and assumptions. For example, decarbonization efforts may be challenged by differing implicit assumptions regarding the acceptability of nuclear power as an alternative.

Failures of Number

If a cause does not reach sufficient scale (or, in the early stages, if participants do not believe that it can), it will not succeed.

- *Narrowness*: Causes that are too narrow to address a broad common interest will fail to gather scale. Often an individual cause can be part of a larger cause with broader appeal. Sometimes, therefore, a new initiative is best folded into a broader one.
- *Proliferation*: The larger the number of causes, the less likely that any one cause will gain critical mass. It's common for every change champion to assume that a new, unique initiative is required to fulfill their goals. While less egotistically satisfying, sometimes it is better to follow Ella Baker's injunction to build on an existing initiative rather than start a new one. This can be seen in initiatives to set standards for sustainable forestry – many competing standards are each supported by a subset of stakeholders without any one gaining critical mass.

Failures of Commitment

Change inevitably faces many obstacles and without sustained commitment, and the appearance of commitment, an initiative is unlikely to endure and succeed.

- *Lack of persistence*: While leaders must generally maintain some flexibility in pursuing their goals, showing too much readiness to compromise or move on to the next initiative will undermine perceived commitment and others' willingness to enlist. Enthusiasm flows naturally with the excitement and novelty of a new initiative. The truer test of commitment is when novelty has worn off, ennui has set in, and progress has stalled.[7] Declaring victory too soon based on achieving one or two actions can also stunt a movement's impact.

---

7 https://bcghendersoninstitute.com/fostering-organizational-stamina-2f8c96b15404.

- *Cheap signals*: A vociferous commitment is not necessarily a lasting or a convincing one. Words are cheap, and commitment is better demonstrated by signals that require more sacrifice from those doing the signaling. For example, many leaders endorsed the recent Business Roundtable initiative for businesses to serve a broad set of stakeholders, but companies have differed greatly in the extent to which they have backed this up with actions in areas like environmental and labor rights.[8] "Statements" might help build initial momentum, but they don't necessarily signal the willingness or ability to work through the toughest and most critical aspects of a problem. An example of a credible signal is the voluntary withdrawal of tobacco from CVS stores, in line with their purpose of promoting health. It cost CVS billions of dollars in lost revenues before eventually spurring new health-related growth.
- *"Actionism"*: Organizations can overemphasize being *action-oriented* and invest heavily in the machinery and language of action – including Gantt charts, milestones, project teams, performance metrics, pulse checks, steering committees, and project charters – which can sometimes have the unintended effect of *deflecting* attention and energy away from taking on the toughest tasks. Busy does not necessarily mean effective.

Failures of Diversity

To be successful, a cause needs to demonstrate that it can eventually appeal to a broad audience and this can be inferred from the diversity of current adherents. Lack of diversity early on can undermine a movement.
- *Preaching to the choir*: Causes can sometimes appear to be successful by preaching to a relatively homogeneous audience that is already aligned in its core beliefs. For example, attendees at sustainability events often demonstrate an impressive degree of alignment and conviction. The more stringent test would be to attract the engagement and support of influencers who are disinterested or skeptical of the cause in question.
- *Preaching to the leaders*: Proponents of an initiative may focus their efforts on winning over the top leaders, such as the C-suite or heads of state, or policy makers. However, employees or citizens at all levels will generally be the ones amplifying the message and implementing a change or feeling its effects, so if they are not also on board with an initiative, it is unlikely to

---

8 Raghunandan, A., and S. Rajgopal (2020). "Do the Socially Responsible Walk the Talk?" *SSRN*, https://papers.ssrn.com/sol3/papers.cfm?abstract_id=3609056.

succeed. Successful social movements mobilize grass roots as much as grass tops.

Collective Action in a Digital World

Digital technology can transform many physical challenges into information problems, and in so doing, greatly reduce the necessary cost and effort to create change. By leveraging technology, the basic elements of collective change can all be executed more rapidly, at lower cost, with less delay and to broader audiences, including:

- The creation of a change agenda
- Its dissemination
- The coordination of collective action
- The tracking of collective impact
- Collective engagement to evolve the agenda
- The recruitment of new members

However, digital technology does not in itself solve the fundamental challenges of Worth, Unity, Commitment, Number, and Diversity – and in fact it also creates several new challenges.

Lower transaction costs facilitate the proliferation of initiatives and communications, which dilutes the average *worth* of each and makes the challenge of breaking through the information clutter harder. For instance, online petitions have dramatically reduced the friction involved in collecting signatures, which has in turn lowered the perceived impact of individual petitions.

In a world more focused on screens than interpersonal interactions, digital speech acts can be easily confused for effective action and *commitment*. As journalist and author Tom Friedman has remarked, today's digital activism may amount in many cases to little more than "firing digital muskets into the Milky Way."

It's certainly easy to reach a large *number* of followers on digital platforms. But this is counterbalanced by a lower likelihood of deep engagement. We should not mistake likes, clicks, or opens for self-initiated action or lasting commitment.

And the network effects associated with technology are making the world a more polarized place, where affiliation is more tribal in nature and mutual mistrust higher. This increases the risk of preaching only to the converted. While this may give the appearance of *unity*, it can easily mask a failure of *diversity*.

Most social media platforms prioritize content that is in line with preexisting interests, so many users are only exposed to content they agree with. As a result, they can believe that there is a high level of agreement with their opinions, even if they are marginal when viewed from a broader perspective.

Unlocking the Mystery of Collective Action

As corporations grow larger, as our digital reach expands and as business activity encroaches upon social and planetary limits, our challenges are increasingly collective in nature. We cannot apply the convenient, mechanical recipe of "problem-analysis-plan-action" to such challenges. Effective collective action is not simply project management writ large or project management by digital means.

We don't yet have a definitive playbook for effective collective action in an interconnected world, but we can derive some useful principles by extracting lessons from social activism and systems science, and from observing the failure and success of complex change initiatives:

1. Make it easy for someone to act. Instead of focusing mainly on decoding what actions logically need to take place, focus on motivating voluntary action-taking. Understand what people must believe, and how they can be inspired, influenced, or incentivized to change their behaviors. Provide educational platforms, role models, mobile apps, and other support tools to enable people to easily take action toward the desired outcome. For example, the NationSwell Council, a community of service-minded leaders, engages members with "The One Thing" they can do to further a social goal.

2. Convey the *worth* of your initiative by focusing on the purpose underpinning plans and goals. A strongly supported purpose can function as an intrinsic motivator that drives self-initiated behaviors in a much more powerful way than extrinsic motivators.

3. To create *unity*, don't just transmit information but tell stories. Stories can be powerful tools that go beyond facts by creating holistic meaning, assimilability, familiarity, vividness, and emotional appeal. The most emotionally compelling stories include characters, memorable images, lessons, and a call to action.

4. Broaden the *number* of people that support you by building on pre-existing initiatives. This not only ensures that your initiative starts with a significant support base, but it also allows you to leverage existing processes, communities, and resources where appropriate to accelerate impact.

5. Communicate *commitment* by highlighting and celebrating examples of costly signals and pivotal actions. Committing to goals publicly, putting skin in the game and taking on the toughest challenges are costly but effective signals of commitment. In non-profit organizations, the levels of increasing commitment can be made explicit, from being a member, to donating money/time, to advocating for policy change.

6. Realize *diversity* in your support base early on. Communicate with and enlist dissimilar people and skeptics. Create spaces in the agenda for people to add their adaptations consistent with the mission. This increases the chance that your initiative can reach critical mass without later running into resistance from groups with conflicting interests. It might also expand the initiative in creative ways you had not considered.

7. Leverage the unique strengths of technology to sustain new forms of collective action. Use technology platforms to facilitate collective action, but regard it as a "force multiplier" rather than something which guarantees success in its own right. There is no number of clicks or likes which will guarantee that anyone acts. And often the mechanisms of power – such as the legislative process – are decidedly non-digital.

For instance, technology drastically lowers friction for large-scale asynchronous collaboration, which has made initiatives like Wikipedia possible. The Wikimedia foundation catalyzed collective action by developing a clear vision (creating a freely accessible, massively comprehensive encyclopedia) and making crowd-sourced collaboration tools widely available. Volunteers have leveraged these tools to create the largest and most accurate repository of freely available knowledge through bottom-up action.

For movements to sustain over time, the knowledge of the organization's history and outcomes can be archived so present change agents build on their predecessors' success rather than repeating the failures. Similarly, archiving can synchronize sub-communities of action.

8. Lead for Collective Action. There's no collective action without the right leadership. Effective collective action is not brought about by charisma alone, nor by compulsion, fear, or excellence in project management. The jobs to be done in orchestrating collective action include understanding and articulating a common purpose, understanding the mechanisms of power and bottlenecks in a system, communicating in a persuasive manner to a diverse audience, persisting in the face of obstacles, and flexibly evolving approaches as circumstances change. These are likely to demand different traits from those observed in traditional top-down leaders, such as humility, being comfortable in one's own skin, the ability to establish trust with a wide range of personalities, adaptability, integrity, and emotional intelligence. The effective leadership of collective action (Box 13.1) may also need different types of leadership profiles for different stages of a movement or initiative.

Box 13.1: Putting It All Together: 96 Elephants

The Wildlife Conservation Society's "96 Elephants" campaign is an example of a successful initiative that combines many of the elements discussed in this chapter. Faced with mounting pressure on elephant populations from poaching, the WCS launched the initiative, which was ultimately successful in closing down ivory markets in China and the US, with the active collaboration of both countries. The narrative of saving elephants from extinction was a highly vivid and worthwhile one to a broad audience – likely much more so than had WCS targeted poaching in general. The campaign was focused on simple actions citizens could take like pledging not to buy ivory, writing letters to congressional representatives, or donating funds. One of the masterstrokes of the campaign was to position it as a bilateral issue on which US and China could show unity. The campaign was amplified to reach critical numbers by rolling legislative precedents out across states using templated laws, by being promoted to US citizens via WCS's network of affiliate zoos, and by an official program of factory closures in China. By working legal mechanisms, WCS could ensure that measures were enshrined in law and therefore constituted an enduring commitment. Another key aspect of the campaign was that it focused on uniting very diverse constituencies in a synergistic manner from state legislators, to congressional representatives of both parties, to political leaders in China and US, to African leaders, to regional conservation societies, to ordinary citizens. Finally, while leveraging some digital tools and approaches, WCS was not distracted from the fact that many of the key influence levers in this case – enlisting the support of governors and politicians such as then-Secretary of State, Hillary Clinton, drafting legislation and diplomacy – were decidedly interpersonal. As WCS CEO, Cristián Samper, said "Not everything we do comes together like this, but this was a focus initiative, we were all fully committed to seeing it through and we worked the system from grass roots to grass tops to make sure that the highly diverse stakeholder set was fully united throughout."[9]

---

9 WCS member interviews. The authors are very grateful to the executive staff and board of WCS for the access and time they gave us to discuss and shape this article (Cristián Samper, John Calvelli, Susan Chin, Alejandro Santo Domingo, Rosina Bierbaum, Rudolph Crew, Katie Dolan, Julia Marton-Lefèvre, and Juan Manuel Santos).

Change is becoming more incessant and complex, requiring new approaches that transcend traditional project management. By learning from social activism, especially the focus on creating and propagating the will to act, leaders can more effectively bring about change across a diverse set of stakeholders. In the words of Ella Baker, "The major job was getting people to understand that they had something within their power they could use."

Martin Reeves, Leesa Quinlan, Mathieu Lefèvre, Georg Kell
Chapter 14
How Business Leaders Can Reduce Polarization

Rising political polarization[1] can have serious ramifications for businesses. Companies that speak out on controversial issues can face decreased customer loyalty from those with opposing beliefs, increased internal conflict between employees, or reduced sales from boycotts. Furthermore, taking a public stance can often exacerbate social tensions. For example, after the 2018 school shooting in Parkland, Florida, Delta Air Lines was reported to have eliminated an NRA member discount. Despite affecting very few people, the move further heightened tensions around gun control and prompted state lawmakers to threaten the airline's fuel tax exemptions.[2]

Even so, inaction is not necessarily the better strategy. Polarization can also affect businesses that *do not* speak out, through decreased customer loyalty, market unpredictability caused by public misinformation, or foregone opportunities due to fear of a backlash. Silence can also be perceived as tacit support for one side of an issue. For example, Uber faced a widespread boycott[3] for its reported silence regarding a US travel ban on majority-Muslim countries in 2017, which some viewed as an endorsement of the policy.

These risks are compounded by increasing expectations that companies should practice "corporate statesmanship"[4] by playing a more visible public role in social and political issues. Tellingly, CEOs are split almost evenly[5] on whether to take a public stand on controversial social issues or not.

If both advocating for a position and remaining silent can backfire, what actions *can* CEOs take to effectively reduce division – and protect their businesses in increasingly polarized times?

1 https://www.bcg.com/publications/2021/understanding-business-ramifications-of-social-polarization.
2 https://www.usatoday.com/story/news/2018/03/02/delta-reviews-all-fare-discount-programs-after-nra-dispute-costs-georgia-tax-break/388587002/.
3 https://www.nytimes.com/2017/01/31/business/delete-uber.html.
4 https://www.bcg.com/publications/2018/case-corporate-statesmanship.
5 https://fortune.com/2021/05/18/should-ceos-speak-out-about-controversial-social-and-political-issues-stakeholder-capitalism-ceo-daily/.

Note: This chapter was previously published in the *Harvard Business Review,* October 8, 2021.

https://doi.org/10.1515/9783110775174-014

Bridging the Divide

Instead of focusing on the false binary of simply taking a public stance or stay-ing silent, CEOs would be better off understanding and addressing the *context* of rising polarization and doing so in a strategic manner.

First, Get Your Own House in Order

Before engaging in public debates, leaders should ensure that they have ad-dressed polarization within their own organizations. Not only will this help avoid accusations of hypocrisy, but it will also create a stronger foundation for external influence.

The workplace is one of the few remaining social spaces for repeated inter-group interaction and cooperation. We may bowl alone,[6] but we still work to-gether. Each day, we engage with colleagues who don't necessarily share our social and political views in order to complete a common mission, creating pos-itive connections across lines of difference that may not exist in broader soci-ety. This is a valuable and major source of social cohesion in its own right.

Furthermore, a divisive environment can negatively affect employee senti-ment – and performance. A 2016 survey[7] found that 24% of workers said a divi-sive political environment led to negative work outcomes, including poor work quality and lower productivity. To resolve and avoid these negative effects, leaders can make efforts to bridge gaps and foster cooperation between em-ployee groups in the workplace.

- **Know thyself.** Listen to your employees to better understand their back-grounds, interests, and values – especially across different cultural and geographical groups. Leaders can accomplish this through roundtable dis-cussions, anonymous surveys, and other formats that encourage open communication and feedback from employees. If leaders better under-stand their teams and organizations, they will be better able to address common employee concerns. For example, after software company Base-camp reportedly banned[8] discussions about social and political issues, some 30% of their employees resigned, an outcome that may have been

---

6 http://bowlingalone.com/.

7 https://www.apa.org/news/press/releases/2016/09/employees-political-talk.

8 https://www.nytimes.com/2021/04/30/technology/basecamp-politics-ban-resignations. html.

avoided if leadership had a clearer understanding of what their employees needed or wanted.

- **Adopt a consistent stance.** Explicitly outline your company's philosophy regarding engagement on social issues, and ensure that it is consistent with previously established company policies, values, and purpose. Clear and stable expectations can not only reduce confusion and inappropriate behavior, they also can prevent disappointment by employees who feel the company should be doing more – or less – on social issues or who feel that policies are being inconsistently applied. For example, Starbucks reportedly faced criticism[9] in 2020 when employees noted that Pride clothing was permitted workplace attire while Black Lives Matter clothing was banned. Ultimately, the company reversed the ban and adopted a consistent policy.
- **Create common ground.** Make intergroup contact a core organizational value by building shared identities around apolitical interests. Corporate volunteering programs, which can build a sense of unity around a common social interest, are one powerful lever to create meaningful interactions.[10] For example, the American Red Cross Los Angeles Region created a program[11] to bring together members of different faiths – including Baha'i, Muslim, Christian, and Buddhist – to discuss the shared goal of increasing diversity in blood donations and organizing community blood drives.
- **Foster healthy engagement.** Create clear rules and norms for open discussions that encourage honest and respectful communication – and even disagreement – between employees. Leaders can contribute to productive communication by creating open forums for cross-group engagement, keeping a watchful eye for misinformation, and encouraging civil and inclusive behavior. For example, when Cisco created staff forums to discuss difficult social issues, it also implemented a comment "color spectrum"[12] to provide guidance on how employees can keep conversations respectful.
- **Engage the hidden majority.** Ensure that people with moderate or unexpressed views feel comfortable within the organization. A 2018 study[13]

---

9 https://www.eater.com/2020/6/11/21288519/starbucks-says-employees-cant-promote-black-lives-matter-prompting-boycott.

10 https://www.forbes.com/sites/wesgay/2016/11/03/4-reasons-why-a-corporate-volunteer-program-is-a-smart-investment/?sh=5df465633364.

11 https://www.redcross.org/local/california/los-angeles/about-us/news-and-events/press-releases/red-cross-empowers-communities-of-faith-through-preparedness-at-.html.

12 https://www.greatplacetowork.com/resources/blog/how-1-world-s-best-workplace-cisco-showed-the-courage-to-connect-in-2020.

13 https://hiddentribes.us/media/qfpekz4g/hidden_tribes_report.pdf.

placed 67% of Americans in the "Exhausted Majority," who say they feel fatigued by politics and feel forgotten in current debates. These employees may feel unwelcome in a highly politicized environment. For example, Starbucks faced criticism in 2015 after encouraging customers to discuss racial issues[14] with employees, many of whom felt uncomfortable having such discussions at work but may have felt unable to refuse. As then-CEO Howard Schultz later commented, "These discussions needed to be had, but not in the way we had them."[15] Leaders can create a safe and respectful environment in which these individuals do not feel pressured to adopt a public or artificial stance.

Influence Your Ecosystem

CEOs can have a degree of direct influence over the behavior of customers, suppliers, and other stakeholders within their external business ecosystem. Through these relationships, leaders can broaden their influence and impact, especially on issues of common interest. A strong ecosystem can amplify the expression and realization of a company's purpose and afford expanded possibilities to address the context of polarization.

- **Communicate a clear purpose.** A company's purpose[16] is the bridge between its internal aspirations and capabilities and its external impact, including its ability to address polarization. However, relying mainly on media soundbites or social media posts to communicate purpose can backfire; people are more likely to misunderstand ambiguously brief or ill-defined statements. Fortunately, leaders can easily engage in richer interactions with a company's immediate stakeholders. When engaging with customers and external stakeholders, leaders should also ensure that they use terminology that is simple and easy to understand. For example, Ben & Jerry's includes clear definitions of the issues they support on their website,[17] which helps prevent confusion or misinterpretation.
- **Ensure respectful interactions.** Fighting misinformation is not enough to reduce polarization if the tone of public communication is hostile. More in

---

14 https://www.nytimes.com/2015/03/23/business/media/starbucks-ends-tempestuous-initiative-on-race.html.
15 https://www.businessinsider.com/howard-schultz-failed-race-together-campaign-2019-1.
16 https://hbr.org/2019/09/put-purpose-at-the-core-of-your-strategy.
17 https://www.benjerry.com/values/issues-we-care-about.

Common[18] is an organization that develops initiatives to address fracturing within society. Its research suggests that 70% of Germans[19] and 86% of French people[20] are concerned about increasingly hateful public rhetoric. Business leaders can influence how stakeholders interact – at least on company-run platforms – and can reduce antagonism by preventing the use of toxic or polarizing language. Twitter recently developed a feature[21] that detects and flags "mean" messages before they are sent. During tests, these flags reportedly prompted 34% of people to change or delete their messages and to write 11% fewer offensive messages going forward.

– **Develop like-minded coalitions.** Companies are increasingly aligning around issues like workplace behavior norms, DE&I (diversity, equity, and inclusion) commitments, and climate change efforts. By working together, firms not only magnify their influence and impact, but they can also exchange and leverage new skills and tactics to combat rising polarization. For example, the News Media Alliance, a bipartisan alliance of news media organizations, collaborates to make policy recommendations and advocate for a free and independent press.[22]

– **Invest in new solutions.** Leaders can combat polarization by investing in new platforms, tools, or concepts that directly address the context of rising polarization, both within and beyond the corporation. These solutions may include techniques for increasing effective collaboration between groups or for identifying and highlighting common traits. For example, companies can contribute to organizations that support deliberation across different groups to help reduce polarization. One such organization is America In One Room, a Stanford-based group that facilitates political debate[23] across a diverse and representative sample of the American population.

18 https://www.moreincommon.com/our-work/what-we-do/.

19 https://www.dieandereteilung.de/media/o5konmo3/more-in-common_fault-lines_executive-summary.pdf.

20 https://www.lafranceenquete.fr/.

21 https://www.npr.org/2021/05/06/994138707/want-to-send-a-mean-tweet-twitters-new-feature-wants-you-to-think-again.

22 https://www.newsmediaalliance.org/advocacy/.

23 https://cdd.stanford.edu/2019/america-in-one-room/.

Inspire Broader Impact

The public's rising trust in business[24] – and declining trust in public institutions – means that CEOs can use their public standing to facilitate broader social change. However, individual leaders should maximize their credibility and influence by focusing on a few specific areas of interest and expertise that are consistent with their own companies' beliefs and actions and are supported by others in their ecosystems. Furthermore, leaders will have more ability to shape emerging issues than those that are already highly polarized. Conversely, diving reactively into well-developed controversies – especially where they have not put their own house in order – can be risky and damaging.

– **Promote fact-based discourse.** Companies should support their own communications with independently verified facts, while promoting the cause of independent, fact-based journalism. These actions can help to prevent the spread of misinformation among employees and within society more broadly. Furthermore, companies can avoid doing business with known purveyors of misinformation. For example, multiple companies reportedly pulled their advertising from Facebook in 2020 for its perceived delays in halting the spread of misinformation[25] on its platform.

– **Catalyze inclusive communities.** Leaders can reduce antagonism and increase intergroup understanding by taking actions such as investing in inclusive marketing techniques or creating public forums and events for cross-group interactions. Large majorities of people in western democracies say they are exhausted by the division in society.[26] CEOs could tap into this desire for unity by promoting intergroup contact in public communications and actions. This is what Danish broadcaster TV2 did by making the promotion of social cohesion a major part of its public image.[27]

– **Build international bridges.** Business has become increasingly global, and many companies have economic relationships with customers, suppliers, and investors across international borders. Leaders can use their international footprints to connect diverse regions and grow their stakeholder communities to encompass a broader range of perspectives. For example,

---

24 https://www.edelman.com/trust/2021-trust-barometer.
25 https://www.nytimes.com/2020/06/26/business/media/Facebook-advertising-boycott.html.
26 https://www.moreincommon.com/attitudes-toward-democracy/.
27 https://www.thenorthalliance.com/our-work/all-that-we-share/.

Microsoft involves corporate volunteers[28] in its African technology education program,[29] providing a shared experience for individuals from different countries and further developing local relationships. This interaction across borders is a potentially powerful lever against a newly resurgent axis of polarization: geopolitical division and nationalism.

Rising polarization is unlikely to disappear anytime soon, and it can have severe ramifications for businesses, whether they take a public stance or not. However, by taking a selective and strategic approach, CEOs can reduce the harm of polarization first within their own companies, and then within their broader communities by focusing on issues and situations where they have self-interest, credibility, and influence.

---

28 https://www.devex.com/news/why-your-company-needs-an-international-corporate-volunteering-program-85436.
29 https://query.prod.cms.rt.microsoft.com/cms/api/am/binary/RWCYLh.

List of Figures

https://doi.org/10.1515/9783110775174-015

Index

https://doi.org/10.1515/9783110775174-016

www.ingramcontent.com/pod-product-compliance
Lightning Source LLC
Chambersburg PA
CBHW061325220326
41599CB00026B/5044